Black Mountain

A Collection of Poems

Lesli Birkhead

BALBOA.PRESS

A DIVISION OF HAY HOUSE

Balboa Press books may be ordered through booksellers or by contacting:

Balboa Press
A Division of Hay House
1663 Liberty Drive
Bloomington, IN 47403
www.balboapress.com
1 (877) 407-4847

Because of the dynamic nature of the Internet, any web addresses or links contained in this book may have changed since publication and may no longer be valid. The views expressed in this work are solely those of the author and do not necessarily reflect the views of the publisher, and the publisher hereby disclaims any responsibility for them.

The author of this book does not dispense medical advice or prescribe the use of any technique as a form of treatment for physical, emotional, or medical problems without the advice of a physician, either directly or indirectly. The intent of the author is only to offer information of a general nature to help you in your quest for emotional and spiritual well-being. In the event you use any of the information in this book for yourself, which is your constitutional right, the author and the publisher assume no responsibility for your actions.

Any people depicted in stock imagery provided by Getty Images are models, and such images are being used for illustrative purposes only. Certain stock imagery © Getty Images.

Print information available on the last page.

ISBN: 978-1-9822-4094-3 (sc)
ISBN: 978-1-9822-4096-7 (hc)
ISBN: 978-1-9822-4095-0 (e)

Library of Congress Control Number: 2020900357

Balboa Press rev. date: 01/15/2020

Contents

CHAPTER TWO – THE TRAVELER SERIES

CHAPTER THREE

CHAPTER FOUR - JEFF

CHAPTER FIVE

Preface

Prior to writing this book I had written other works of poetry but never kept them. When I started writing the poems in this book I began letting others read them which is something I had not done in the past. I was encouraged that my words could help others. With that, I was off and writing. I felt that if I could even help one person then that would be very rewarding.

My first poem, The Uniform, was written after seeing a veteran who suffered from PTSD after losing a leg in Iraq. I tend to put myself in the position of those whose stories inspire me and I write from my heart. Inspiration comes in many forms including what I see and hear. While I often write in the first person, most of the poems and their content are fiction and not about my personal experiences. Some are abstract and others are fantasy. I do believe that readers in general can relate to the content of many of the poems.

I consider my style interpretive because I write from a certain perspective. However, it is left to the individual to interpret a poem as they will. There's no right or wrong. Some poems are written in a series. I call those a fantasy novel by poetry.

Writing poetry is very cathartic. I feel a sense of satisfaction and accomplishment when I complete a poem.

While I try to include a positive or even a spiritual spin, some of the poems are rather dark and even discuss thoughts of suicide and suicide itself. I do not in any way condone suicide but I also know the reality and the impact that it has on others. I have felt the personal pain of life and the personal pain of someone committing suicide. If you are having suicidal thoughts or are planning suicide, please talk to someone. Call 911 or the national suicide hotline at 1-800-273-8255 or text CONNECT to 741741 from anywhere in the USA.

Dedication

A special dedication to Jeff T, Alan, Robert (Bobby) D, Henry (Carl) C, and Ron K. I pray you have found the peace you could not find on earth.

I dedicate this to those who have and are suffering and who are victims or survivors of past and current atrocities, bullying, physical and mental illness, addiction in all forms, as well as those touched by adversity and any other demons that may be causing sorrow, pain, or unhappiness.

I pray that all of you find peace and live with freedom in your heart and mind.

I also pray that man's inhumanity to animals and sea animals also ends.

I want to thank my family for their support and encouragement, especially to Julie and Jay without whom I could not have begun or finished this project. A special thank you to DR, JR, JS, CO for your support, friendship and loyalty through the years. A thank you to DB who showed me the lighter side of life. And to JW for listening to all my stories for years!

A special thank you to all current and former members of the military. Thank you for your sacrifice and service which allows my freedom.

A portion of the proceeds of the sale of this book and ebook will go to the following organizations:

Save the Whales
The Humane Society of the United States
Hope for the Warriors
ASPCA

CHAPTER ONE

The Uniform

I'm not a killer
That's just not me
But I had to do it
It was him or me

It was my job
But down deep inside
Was I trying
To justify

I was angry
At the terror they brought
In the name of freedom
They had to be stopped

I looked though the scope
And I did not see
The one in the crosshairs
As a human being

Somehow the khakis
Made it okay
The bastard won't see
Another day

When on the line
Muscle memory
Don't think, just act
Incoming

I can hear my heart
And the horror's real
I just played the part
But there's so much fear

When I took a life
I didn't see the blood
But locked inside
Was an emotional flood

I talked to myself
As I tried to survive
It's just a movie
Compartmentalize

Away from the front
Time to reflect
My soul hurts
For the senseless deaths

It was more than that
Internally
There was a conflict
It's hard to breathe

A flash, a pop
I hit the ground
Can't even tolerate
A normal sound

And the nightmares
Nearly every night
Wake in a sweat
I'm in the fight

I don't feel safe
And my mind plays games
I think I'm going
To go insane

3

I used to have
A normal mind
Now it's outta my hands
And I'm wracked with fright

But my chin is up
Though I've been changed
The scars I carry
My mind in chains

I hope to find the mental key
And allow myself to be reborn
Learning to walk all over again
Though I wore a uniform

Black Mountain

Black Mountain is a place
That I go to in my mind
When I'm feeling lost or lonely
Or to leave the daily grind

That is where I go
When I'm feeling down
Or when I'd rather take my life
I go there til I'm found

I may end up going for an hour
Or maybe for a year
I have to stay til 'it' is all gone
'It' is all my fear

Fear of facing things head on
Fear of facing reality
Fear of facing pain and loss
Fear of facing what makes me me

My thoughts cause chaos in my mind
And they intrude upon my day
If I take things a breath at a time
Relaxed and grounded I can stay

This is my friend the black mountain
No judgment or hatred from anyone else
A safe place where I can gain my strength
Just a way of taking care of myself

The Veil Disease

There's no dusting off the life
Or the cobwebs in the mind
A condition full of strife
The veil disease defined

A place where memories go
And get lost in the dark spaces
Experiences are new yet again
As are beloved people
and places

Like when a shooting star
Appears through the Milky Way
A memory may come through
Though brief and will not stay

Misfortune and affliction
A world of disparity
The veil disease steals
from families
With one's fading
moments of clarity

The veil it hangs low
Over the mind not the face
Awareness and
memories frozen
In its unending haze

There's a blindness of memories
And a seeing without
recognition
A knowing without
comprehension
And a doing with
much confusion

It's high noon with no shadows
There's no taking time to see
Not even a concept
of time itself
Nor a rapture to set one free

The mind's not there
but the body is
What makes them them
is gone for good
A transitioning for
all the universe
A shell remains where
greatness stood

Nothing's clear with
the veil disease
A perpetual opening
of the lions' gate
What once was old is new again
Is it all a blank or a blank slate

Through the Darkness

I don't have the
strength to call out
Or the energy to climb out
Or the vision to see a way out
Do I even want out?

I'm here in this deep dark hole
Maybe this is my new role
However this is taking its toll
Suicide, it is my goal

I make the plans to do the deed
Even to which day of the week
Soon my mind will be freed
Now courage is all I need

Anxiety, illness, feeling low
I've felt this way so long I know
No ambition to try so I forgo
Any attempt to feel or grow

But could this feeling
ever go away
Could I still be the
kid that played
One last time I decide to pray
God give me the
strength to stay

I have to be willing to
take the first step
To have the courage
to move ahead
Give me hope, take
away the dread
I don't really want
to end up dead

Through the darkness
I think I see
A flash of light ahead of me
It's just so hard to let
go and believe
No more holding the
bars that I create

The Ride

Take a ride on a horse
Short Cut or Black Night
Delilah will lead the way
They are a mighty sight

Along the way
Things may get rough
But face it all together
The three of you are tough

You may need a little nudge
If you're stuck on the trail
As long as you go forward
You will not fail

The ride will be bumpy
From time to time
But take in the beauty
And look for a sign

This is where you are
Where do you want to go
Make your decision
At times you'll take it slow

The smell of fresh air
Clears your mind to see
You can pause anytime
And that is where you'll be

You'll see the signs
As you ride along
Just keep trotting forward
Now you can't go wrong

The right place and right time
Curiously
Along your chosen trail
Lies your destiny

The view of the horizon
Let things be as they may
It is what you make it
Today is a new day

The Smile

You always see me smile
Because I don't want you to see
What's really going on inside
You'll think of me differently

I feel such total torment
A discomfort from within
Though I remain outgoing
And maintain a goofy grin

I know that I cannot even think
That my minds not completely
right
I'm so afraid I'll break down
Alone and unable to fight

As time goes on and days
pass by
It's just like second nature
To keep from you the truth about
My longstanding mental failure

Without the happy face I show
I'd have to deal with the scary
stuff
So try as I may I hide the truth
Life with myself is really tough

Ignoring the part of me that's
real
There's daily slough of my mind
and self
I don't understand and
nothing's clear
So I concentrate on someone else

Show the opposite of how I feel
And never letting you see through
I'm scared and fear I'll disappear
Denial as my torment grows

When I allow my mind to view
And I start to analyze
None of it makes any sense
I have no choice but to deny

I get to a point and face my fear
But the me I know has faded away
Unable to handle the change
within
Realizing death is the only way

"Never let them see you cry"
And "weakness never show"
To hell with that cuz in this life
They're needed to help you grow

When smiling through the pain
Becomes too much to bear
Remember you are not alone
With others you can share

Mental illness is not a choice
And can happen randomly
Sometimes you see it coming
Others suffer silently

It's okay that you're ill
And it's okay to break the smile
It's okay if you want to give up
But only for a while

Just keep on being tough
Tougher than the illness that
you face
There are many options
Death is not the only way

I know the pain's unbearable
It worsens when you don't
believe
Help could be just around the
corner
Though thoughts of death
bring imagined peace

There's so many people
Who would do anything for you
But you have to reach out
So they can see you through

Even the epitome of happiness
Can have demons that arise
The challenge is to face them
Not to run away and hide

When you think you have no
choice
Give it another try
We are more alike than different
Together we'll fight the fight

Get comfortable in your own skin
Though there's chaos in your
mind
Be okay with who you are
And to yourself be kind

The Painted Lady

She was a painted lady
But not along the coastal town
Not a song sung by an icon
The cops had brought her down

She had just been painting
When the voices changed their tune
She colored herself purple
The cops would be there soon

Who would arrive to help her
She had been labeled mentally ill
Would they want to harm her
For her this thought was real

Some people had been following her
For many many days
She hadn't slept for a week
At least that's what she'd say

When help got to her
Would they be nice or not care
She didn't want to hurt anyone
She was just confused and scared

When receiving the right treatment
She'd feel a lot more calm
And maybe with a little luck
The voices would be gone

The Mask

The devil wears
The angels mask
Deception
His only task

He speaks in harmony
With dripping venom
The illusive demon
And undiscerning victims

Never knowing
The game of con
Ignorant
To what's right or wrong

He hopes to convince one
With his mask
For with gifts of favor
Sincerity lacks

Continue the game
When the deck is stacked
Look for the rainbow
Though now it's white and black

Color not
No shades of grey
Evil won't cease
When he gets his way

Downward one spirals
As he removes his mask
And laughs below
In the fire he basks

But the mortal man
Within you resides
And intuition
Is not blind

So convincing
Of an archangels light
Steadfastly grounded
He cannot take flight

One's inner voice
A warning heeds
Unveil a cross
When evil meets

Bring the color of confidence
To a jaded fool
And skip the dance
The devils reuse

A charming nature
Don't take the bait
Or in hell you'll live out
Your eternal fate

The Demon

The demon led you down the
alley
Promising you a trip
He knew that this time
Your wings would be clipped

He started the conversation
"Take a walk with me
I'll show you the other side
A better place to be"

Because of the pain you were in
And considering where you stood
The thought of a better place
Really sounded good

He showed you some familiar
tapes
Hurtful times from your past
Times when you did something
wrong
And good times that didn't last

He continued to play more
mind games
As the projector rolled the film
The demon won't stop
badgering you
You're more than overwhelmed

He wanted you to feel worse
And fill your mind with guilt
Not giving you the chance to
remember
The good life that you had built

He showed you things to help
his cause
Then he brought you to the edge
The demon doesn't want to
help you
He just wants you dead

Things can only get better
When they can't get any worse
Though your pain is so
overwhelming
Don't fall for the demons curse

I do not have the answers
But there certainly is One who
might
At times it's not what we want
to hear
But the demons we have to fight

At first this was a one way walk
But you can always change your
mind
Get help and ask for strength
And believe things will change
in time

There's always something worth
living for
It may not seem so in times of
strife
But giving up is not the end of
misery
It's just the start in another's life

The Journey

I see you falling to your knees
Crying out no God please
Don't take this one from me
The end of a journey

I saw your eyes so empty
How could you still believe
In a God so faithfully
Stuck on a journey

The destination doesn't see
That which makes us free
There's life in the in-between
It's your journey

Like a river or a stream
Here until eternity
We live on in those we teach
The beginning of the journey

It's not the destination or the
journey
Or all the time thinking and
worrying
A self-fulfilling prophecy
Humility or Journey

Perhaps love may be the key
Or an inner beauty
That makes one happy
During the journey

Do eyes allow you to see
Is it a stick or redwood tree
It's all in what you perceive
Part of the journey

A gift that you can't keep
Remember just to breathe
Can we find serenity
Along the journey

The limits of the minds capacity
We make our own reality
Is there more for us to reach
Just passengers on the journey

The ride it may be bumpy
From ourselves we try to flee
The time has come you must
leave
The end of your journey

In the end what's a memory
Peace of mind will set you free
Take a number and have a seat
The beginning of another
journey

The Gate

As I make my way through
the fog
I see You standing there
At the entrance to the gate
It is You who decides my fate

Letting others in without
question
You closed the gate on me
You asked why You should
let me in
Down to my knees I went

I said, with a tear in my eye
I felt empty deep inside
Alone and lost and feeling for
others too
I curled up and lost my way
to You

I couldn't take Your hand
It may be hard to understand
I thought I had a plan
But I was only human

Then in a loud voice I heard
"I gave you the gift of birth
I was there for you night
and day
Then you seemed to lose your
faith"

I was hurt and in pain
From then on nothing was
the same
I walked alone and in silence I
remained
Just wanting to end the game

"You were never alone
I accompanied you up every hill
I would never abandon you
But I gave you free will"

"What would you do if you had
another chance
Would you reach out and grab
My hand
Would you gather the strength
to believe
Would you have faith in Me"

I trust in You and always have
I see two sets of footprints in
the sand
I have fear but faith if it's not
too late
Will You still let me go through
the gate

"Go now let your new life begin
Do your best until we meet again
Live your dreams and hold on
to your faith
Then you won't fear your fate"

I took a huge sigh of relief
As I turned to leave
I had a question so I looked back
Why did you give me another
chance

He said, "it was you who
decided to try
I am here to be your guide
I promise to be with you
through it all
Even when you stumble and fall"

"Like a bird that is set free
You have the choice or not to
believe
Like wind helping a bird to fly
I am here when you want to cry"

I walked away with a nod
Did I really just talk to God
Will I change or remain the same
Maybe it's all been a mind game

Through the fog and down the
stairs
I woke up for once no
nightmare
A feeling of hope in my soul
But what if I fall in a deep
dark hole

Things will happen that I know
God please just don't let go
Of my hand and hold me tight
Till You show me the bright
white light

One day I'll knock or ring
Your bell
Hoping I climbed out of the hell
Finally arriving at Your gates
I was having fun that's why
I'm late

The Compass

When you're flying through the sky
Concentrate on up ahead
If you turn around
You just might end up dead

If you must take a different route
Remember where you've been
Remember where you're going to
Be on your way again

Sometimes you have to lift your wings
To move forward
But if you do this enough
You will be able to soar

Let your senses be your guide
But if you happen to be lost
You can always find your way
Take out your compass

You'll never be off the trail
Cuz the compass points True North
Believe you have it in you
And you'll always move on forth

When it comes to direction
We don't like to ask people
But I know you won't let me down
You are my compass needle

Sometimes you have to let go
Of what's holding you back from moving on
So that you can hold onto
What matters til it's gone

The Darkness Lurks

Does the darkness ever leave
Or do we just learn how to ignore it
Is the darkness a way of life
Are we waiting to fall in its pit

Is the darkness a part of us
Hiding just beneath the surface
Waiting for the right moment
When we question our own purpose

When we're sick and tired
And nothing's going right
The darkness looms nearby
When we can no longer fight

Transition to the darkness
Sometimes it's just so easy
Feel it coming then letting go
No more responsibility

Perhaps a nice place to visit
But you don't want to live there
It's damn hard to leave
When in the lions lair

When you see a shadow
Become more enlightened
Because grey can turn to black
When you become frightened

Don't let go but fight it fiercely
Fight it with all your might
Don't let the darkness win you over
It's always darkest before the light

The Face I Wear

Sometimes I feel
I'm made of stone
And the face I wear
Is not my own

I put on a mask
Each day I wake
I fill a role
But my life is fake

Several times
In a given day
I put on
A different face

Getting away
Is what I need
And allow my mind
To be free

But it's all the same
In a different place
I still put on
Another face

Everyone wants
A part of me
So I become
Who they need

All the while
I lose myself
As I've become
Someone else

When the makeup
Is wiped clean
Perhaps then I'll know
What my life means

But for as long
As I wear the mask
I live each day
In someone's past

And these faces
I've always shown
A life I've lived
That's not my own

But why can't I
Just be me
Cuz in the mirror
I'm afraid to see

What's underneath
All the bandages
I wear the masks
So I can manage

Until I change
What I allow
For others needs
I still bow

And the face
I choose to wear
Is just the cross
That I must bear

Trapped

When trapped
And there's no place to run
It's a crime of the mind
When the obsessions come

I sit in a daze
Trapped in time
Eyes open but not seeing
And I'm paralyzed

Trapped in thought
Everything else ceases
Loose cognitions
A box of puzzle pieces

Nothing occupying
My thoughts and mind
Pieces missing
And a shell left behind

Putting it together
Requires being free
But endless obsessions
Hinder ability

One piece at a time
Missing pieces not found
No moving forward
No turning around

While sitting dazed
I need to blink
To see more clearly
And be able to think

Stagnant waiting
An uncertain plot
Trapped in time
Trapped in thought

The Cross to Bear

Suffering and pain
Though not equal or fair
Sometimes injustice
Is the cross that you bear

Affliction or bad fortune
May not be all about you
Perhaps others' observations
Of the things that you do

Alone you'll find no answers
In your quest and analysis
Time to turn it over
And spiritually submit

Your unwavering faith
In the God you trust
Your virtue maintained
Though you've had enough

Job did shave his head
And he suffered great
Not even the trials given him
Could ever shake his faith

"Is that all
You've got for me"
Sometimes a test
Is what we need

At times God works through us
It's not a punishment
And ones' evil motivation
May not make any sense

The devil stays busy
Pushing you to explode
So find strength Beyond
And in the Book of Job

The Color of Depression

You see beauty
I see green
You see a flower
I just see leaves

You see a blue sky
I see clouds
I feel alone
When in a crowd

You speak the words
But there is no sound
There's no tick tock
When the clock is wound

I begin to wonder
What might be wrong
Cuz you hear the music
But I hear no song

I see darkness
You see light
Who decides
Which one is right

Is it all
In one's perception
Is it the rule
Or the exception

The poetry ended
No more rhymes
No more thoughts
Of good times

Is the glass half empty
Or is it half full
Are you just covering your eyes
With proverbial wool

We see things differently
So is there something wrong
Is one weak
And the other strong

Are you critical
Or maybe sad
Perhaps depressed
Tearful or mad

Getting motivated
May seem difficult
But you'll feel better
If you get help

Depression shows up in various ways and forms. For some people, there are no outward signs. These individuals may maintain a happy appearance. For others depression can be paralyzing.

If you suffer from depression or think you are, speak up and don't go it alone. And if you think you know someone who is depressed encourage them to seek help. Be there for them. Sometimes those in a depressed state not only need to be thrown a life preserver but need to be pulled from the grip of depression.

Don't ever, ever give up! You do not have to go it alone. You are not alone!

The Boogeyman

I kept a nightlight on cuz I was scared
I thought it came from my nightmares

But as I opened my eyes slowly
In the darkness loomed possibilities

My mind plays tricks and makes me see
The things I'm afraid of- that I create

The thoughts inside alter reality
The basis for what I believed

A foundation of fear and insecurities
Real is only what the mind perceives

Facts or not, imagination grows
An open closet at bedtime, anxiety shows

I close my eyes it's late at night
The shadow knows my every fright

When I lay down, my face I hide
And sit up fast when I realize

The boogeyman underneath my bed
Is really here in my head

The Cell

There's no outsiders
When battling my demons
A dark place no doubt
And a lonely feelin'

I adventure into
The padded cell of my mind
Reality or perception
Confusion's what I find

Is it that reality
Is it just a state of mind
Or is it that perception
Is so much more sublime

It's a crime of the mind
The sadness that I feel
Stealing away my peace
And what I believe is real

Perhaps the padded cell
Keeps me from going insane
Safely locked up tight
Will freedom ever reign

And those locking bars
Keeping everything inside
Are really straight jackets
The buckles can't be pried

And the cobwebs they collect
In the corners of my mind
Things I'd rather just forget
Little remnants left behind

Hope is locked away
When the mind it likes to hide
But the key is on the wall
And within arms reach just
outside

No dusting off of life
As the demon dual goes on
And the baggage drags behind
Damn the minds swan song

Lifting of the barbells
The mind will become strong
There's light within the darkness
The demons are all gone

Texting to Homelessness

I was once an executive
In a big house I used to live
Now look at me, look at me

I used to get up at quarter to four
Get ready for the day, leave in
my new sports car
Now look at me, look at me

Hair blowin' in the wind in the
convertible
Even in the rain I would do it still
Now look at me, look at me

Pull into the lot toss the keys
to Joe
Grab a cup of coffee while on
the go
Now look at me, look at me

Take the elevator up to 23
When the doors would open i'd
feel free
Now look at me, look at me

One bad mistake brought me to
my knees
Phone in hand one moment
then a crashing memory
Now look at me, look at me

Officer Bill appalled said you're
so disgusting
Killing that girl cuz you were
texting
Now look at me, look at me

The family was left in utter pain
And pictures of the crash left
me insane
Now look at me, look at me

A fancy home a great job a real
nice car
All traded in for these metal bars
Now look at me, look at me

After 17 years I was let outta
the pen
I am on the streets now a
homeless man
Now look at me, look at me

Once a millionaire, now can you
spare a dime
I just got outta jail I did my time
Now look at me, look at me

I lost my family and my
self-respect
I used to carry a briefcase and
be an exec
Now look at me, look at me

Life can change so quickly even
on a dime
When you're not watching it'll
change your life
Look at me, look at me

No jacket or shoes and I push
a cart
A cardboard bed now I play the
part
Look at me, look at me

Why didn't I pull over to read
that text
'It won't happen to me' now
there'll be no next
Look at me, look at me

Leave your phone alone when
you're behind
the wheel
It can ruin lives and some
won't heal
Look at me, look at me.

Suicide

I grab onto you
With my insidious grip

Before long
You're on a trip

Down you go
Into the deep dark well

You've fallen under
My beguiled spell

You're not weak
But I make you see

You're better off
Following me

I can bring you
Infamous fame

And at the very least
Relief from pain

I can control you
With my allure

And make you see
All of your failures

No matter your adversity
Thoughts or beliefs

I can convince you
Of eternal relief

Sadness, depression
Upset with guilt

I shake the foundation
That you have built

I swoop in
When you can't cope

You're lonely or angry
Or have no hope

I become from taboo
A fantasy

And all you want
Is to be free

I'm what you think about
All the time

Desperation and relief
You feel sublime

I have an agenda
I'm selfish and strong

I'm powerful and convincing
Your troubles are gone

If you don't thwart
You're stuck in my grasp

I'll wipe it out
Your entire past

Once you decide
Then I can begin

I've conned you too
My latest victim

Because if you don't
Cast me aside

You're all mine
I'm Suicide

Suicide is not glamorous. It hurts. It hurts and affects everyone you know and even those you don't know. The thought of suicide or dying or taking your own life may seem like the answer, may seem like relief, may even seem like a welcome alternative to whatever is going on or what you are feeling or going through. The thing is, most of the time choosing life instead will eventually bring about a change or shift or another answer that you will be comfortable with. And, perhaps, your sticking around is to benefit or help someone else, albeit difficult to see this at the time. Life is not always about you but what you bring to someone else, maybe someone you don't even know right now. Trust in this thing called life. It's been around for a very long time and our very nature wants us to live. Sure it may seem "easier" to submit to suicide then to continue with what the issue, problem, or feeling is. But if you fight and continue to fight and even fight again and again, and then fight some more, although you may be absolutely and completely exhausted there will be a shift. Perhaps this shift will not be immediately known to you and will be instead for someone else. But stay open to the workings of the universe and eventually you may see the beauty and goodness that you bring by choosing life.

Suicide wants you. Suicide uses you. Suicide controls you. Suicide tricks you. Suicide convinces you of things that are not so. Suicide wants to win. Period. Don't let it win! DO NOT LET IT WIN!

If you are feeling suicidal or sad or depressed or fearful or destined or defeated or desperate or like you are being called by it or feel like it's an answer or you just want to end it, tell someone, call a hotline, call the suicide hotline at **1-800-273-8255**, call a hospital, call 911 or text CONNECT to 741741 from anywhere in the USA, anytime, about any type of crisis.

Speak up. Do not suffer in silence. You are not alone. YOU ARE NOT ALONE. JUST DON'T DO IT. SURVIVE WHATEVER THE ADVERSITY IS. NO MATTER WHAT DO NOT GIVE UP. DO NOT GIVE IN. FIGHT!

Trapped in Time

When you're trapped
And there's no place to run
It's a crime of the mind
When the obsessions come

I sit and daze
Trapped in time
Not even a word
Comes to mind

Just a thought
Here and there
How much more of this
Can I bear

Nothing occupies
My mind or thoughts
But it's so overwhelming
What the darkness brought

Mean people and bullies
Those who do bad things
Heartache and loss
Their hatred brings

And stupid people
Ought to be banned
As well as others
Who don't give a damn

Taking advantage
Of systems and people
Molesters and pedophiles
They're just plain evil

Criminals and murderers
And those who don't care
The good totally outnumbered
Because the bad are
everywhere

When will it end
Oh yeah it never will
Because in their sadism
They find a thrill

And yet they continue
When they know it's wrong
No good, lazy and hurtful
On earth they don't belong

My empathic anger and agony
Makes it dark inside
So much I can't stand it
This evil I want to fight

But how do you fight someone
You can't even get at
Numb yourself good
And just turn your back

A way to live without
Knowing or feeling the pain
But down deep you know
Someone is a victim again

Not doing anything
The guilt of neglect
Fooling yourself
Cuz there no way to forget

I really don't know
What I can do to help
Perhaps my voice
Will ease someone's hell

It sure isn't much
But it's all that I've got
I'm trapped in time
And trapped in thought

Spirit Guide

Sometimes a spirit guide
Comes to visit us
At times there's a reason
Other times it's just because

Don't look for white feathers
Or a being with wings
But look for the insight
Your spirit guide will bring

When the guide visits
They'll be in disguise
They may stay a while
Or just pass by

They may just be checking
To make sure you're okay
Or they may have come down
To show you a new way

A way to be better
Or a lesson to learn
When they go back to Heaven
It's for you to discern

It may not be obvious
For you the first day
As you may just be sad
That they couldn't stay

But one day it'll hit you
And you'll crack a smile
The spirit guide didn't go away
They're with you all the while

You see you're not meant
To continue to be sad
But be mindful of each moment
And each laugh that you had

It's all about being
One with the universe
Though you miss your spirit
guide
And now your heart may hurt

Keep yourself centered
Your guide's up above
Never to leave you
You felt the love

Sitting on a cloud
Watching over you
Take a deep breath
This you'll get through

You met your spirit guide
So you can forge your path
Pave your own road now
And stop living in the past

The Darkness Returns

It's starting to get dark
Though it's light outside
Like a wave overtaking
And a fear that coincides

There's a lack of feeling
As though every part is numb
Left paralyzed
While wanting to just run

A very familiar feeling
When life starts to all turn black
For a while always worrying
That the darkness would
come back

Falling into the hole
Clawing at the sides
Knowing there's no way to
stop it
But still looking for some light

Free falling down and down
Totally frightened
Time wasted previously
When enlightened

A tear of sadness and defeat
Odds against are always
stacked
A desire to find the light
But the shadow always
comes back

And with every breath
Hope starts to fade
One foot nailed to the floor
There's never been another way

'Progress' always leads back to
this place
Where happiness is robbed
High up on a mountain
Then living always stops

Sitting at the bottom
With darkness all around
There's no way but up from here
Though no ladder to be found

Seeing With the Mind's Eye

Open your awareness
And sense being free
It's kind of like flying
When you're in a dream

It's such a rush
Of feeling good
It'll help you relax
And change your mood

When you become one
With the space all around
You see things clearer
And a good feeling abounds

Practice will enable you
To clear your mind
And a higher level
Of awareness you'll find

There's stuff in the air
That you cannot see
It's not just wind
In the air that you breathe

It's important to believe
In possibilities
Not just the tangible
But mental ability

Allow yourself
To conceptualize
Thoughts and visions now clear
With the mind's eye

Reluctant & Reticent

Reluctant and reticent
I turn my case over
Everything meaningful
Changed forever

What may be important
In the scheme of things
Defines the future
And what it brings

Dressed in pajamas
Day and night
They were white and blue
With a vertical stripe

We were crammed in a room
To take a shower
But there was no soap
And there was no water

How could anyone
Be so callous
And treat human beings
With such malice

Staying neutral
You might've got shot
But going along with them
Now you'll answer to God

A bully to start
A devil inside
Others thought
He was a charismatic guy

Just goes to show
The power of words
Go with intuition
Not by what you heard

He kept his hands clean
But with a stroke of his pen
Innocent people were killed
Again and again

Feeling omnipotent
He treated others so cruelly
But absolute power
Corrupts absolutely

We cannot forget
These atrocities
For if we do
We repeat history

Letting history be your guide
And knowing how you feel
inside
Don't just sit around and bide
your time
Stand up for what you know is
right

Bobby

Like a roller coaster
And it's ups and downs
Mental equilibrium
Can't be found

Try to maintain
Some semblance of sanity
As you try to get through
Another calamity

As the mind sprints
To the cliff of depression
A guilty mind
Walks to confession

You lower the lap bar
And that takes energy
You just want it to end
Mental exhaustion's remedy

It cycles back
For the umpteenth time
That same damn coaster
Begins to take lives

Preceded by times
Of running toward hope
Then being knocked off the
catwalk
Because you can't cope

It's not like you think about
The dip in the ride
But suddenly you're thrown
From side to side

It's nearly impossible
To right yourself
And you don't have the energy
To ask for help

When you know it's a cycle
And not just one round
Your mind feels like it's lost
Never to be found
It's bound to repeat
You know the coaster well
It comes into the station
Then back out to hell

You can't do it again
The chicken exit's right there
So you open the door
And walk down the stairs

At the bottom you find
You think about choices
It's then that you realize
Another rejoices

Nothing is clear
Not your thinking for sure
Choose a different ride
If you can endure

What do you do
When all you see
And all you think about
Is misery

How do you come back
When you're down yet again
How do you begin
When you just want it to end

How do you feel
When you lose a good friend
And when you didn't know
An ear you should lend

There's so much guilt
But you didn't know
Just where their mind
Seemed to go

And the hurt they felt
At the time
When they decided
To suicide

There's never enough answers
For those left to survive
You just wish your friend
Was still alive

You visit his grave
Once in a while
But all you remember
Is his great big smile

Like at the top of the coaster
Where there's a big drop
I just want to exit
Please make it stop

Sorry is something
I never got to say
But hopefully
I'll get to someday

====================

Was it something I said
That helped him decide
To take his life
On that fateful night

And for his friend
A message left behind
I've taken the pills
My body you'll find

What he didn't know
Was how much he was loved
The guilt we all feel
But you're as free as a dove

More than thirty years
Since your desperate act
I have to guess
Cuz I don't know the facts

You suffered in silence
Till you made it end
I wish I could go back in time
To save my friend

A Whales Love

My baby's dead
How do I let go
If I do
There's no more hope

The agony
That I'm feeling
Sends me to the depths
Reeling

Death
Has stolen my reason
And has left me
In utter grievance

I lift you up
Please don't leave me
Oh God please
Just breathe

On my back forever
I cannot let you go
I'll carry you with me
I can't leave you alone

Mile after mile
Wave after wave
Going on without you
I'm big but not brave

My heart aches so much
Not for me but for you
Where will you go all alone
In this great big blue

I carried you
For as long as I could
If I could bring you back
You know that I would

Oh my God I'm so sorry
I couldn't save my babe
I breach for a moment
Then dive with a wave

At the bottom I float along
Missing you so deeply
My heart's still aching
My being in agony

Maybe someday
This agony will lift
And I'll understand
How you were a gift

But that doesn't negate
The pain that has been
The moments since
I let go of your fin

Bird story

Two baby birds were born. They were sibling brothers growing in the nest together. One was beautifully colored with shades of blue, purple, and green. It had facial markings that almost made it look as though it were smiling. The other baby bird was brown, black, and white. The mother bird always took care to fully feed the brightly colored baby bird, while the brown, black and white bird did not get that kind of attention from the mother bird. In fact, the brown, black, and white bird had to feed itself the leftover scraps. The mother bird would often spend time telling the brightly colored bird how beautiful he was and she even groomed him. The brown, black, and white bird groomed himself and did not receive such compliments from the mother bird.

One day the brown, black, and white bird started in on the brightly colored bird. "You think you're all that because you are beautiful and you're always smiling, you don't have a care in the world! Also, mom always pays more attention to you, feeding you and bathing you."

The brightly colored bird said to the brown, black, and white bird "things aren't always as they seem."

The brown, black, and white bird countered, "easy for you to say. You are beautiful and mom gives you everything."

The brightly colored bird said, "beauty is simply what you perceive it to be. It's all in your perception. I've always thought of us as equals and it is not until now that I realize that not to be true. I guess realization too is just perception."

Bewildered, the brown,black,and white bird asked, "what are you talking about?"

The brightly colored bird began.... "when we were born I perceived us as being very much alike in every way. I thought mom fed and groomed us both and in reality she was helping you, preparing you, getting you ready to fly out of this nest, experience the world, find a mate, make a nest of your own and have a family. You get to have it all!"

The brown, black, and white bird said "you get to have it all too. Why was I treated differently?"

The brightly colored bird exclaimed, "you weren't treated differently. I was. When you get ready to fly from this nest, I can't go with you. I don't get to experience the world or find a mate. I can never leave this nest! I cannot see. I was born blind. If I leave this nest I won't know which way is up or where there might be a mountain that I'll slam into."

Suddenly the brown, black, and white bird realized that his brother, the beautiful brightly colored bird was right. While the brightly colored bird may have had coloring that made him beautiful, he didn't know he was any different. In fact, his brother the brightly colored bird thought they were equals in every way. It was only through the brown, black, and white birds perception of favoritism that made the brightly colored bird aware that he didn't have 'vision' but he could 'see' things through his perception. The brightly colored bird had an insight that probably would not have been realized had he not been born blind.

The moral of the story: reality, whether perceived or not may or may not be the same as someone else's reality. It doesn't make one right over the other, it just makes them unique.

Oh, and in case you were wondering what happened with the birds, well, the brown, black, and white bird eventually left the nest. He found a mate and brought that mate back to the nest he shared with his brother where the three of them lived happily ever after.

Crystal Ball

Although there's no crystal ball
There still may be some shards
To put together like a puzzle
And determine when life will be hard

Hopefully there's some peace
In those shards of glass
Maybe to inspire you
When hope is all but dashed

Would you let the gypsy
Tell you who you are
Why believe a different story
When you know yours in your heart

Life takes us to strange places
And sometimes you have no say
Though trials and tribulations
May help get you through someday

It may be what you're handed
On your knees you may ask why
Don't take too long to figure it out
This is your only life

If you could see the future
What would be the view
The pieces are now arranged
Held together with lots of glue

Enjoy the moment where you are
Don't use the rear view mirror
Go to where you want to be
In this seat you get to steer

Please Listen

I was strolling through the
courtyard
And from above I heard a "hi"
A young girl leaning on the
window screen
She couldn't have been more
than five

She pressed against that barrier
So hard it left a dent
I asked her please step back
Then I asked her once again

But she just kept on talking
Though it was not her words
What got me was this little girl
Just wanted to be heard

I thought how many more
like her
Were not heard but only seen
How many others like her
Had dented all their screens

I wondered if she ever shed a tear
For not being listened to
I wondered if her parents
Even had a clue

There's many people out there
Who surely can relate
Hopefully they will find an ear
Before it gets too late

So many have a story
If someone gives them the time
Many want to feel they're heard
Or they slowly die inside

Thoughts, needs, ideas, wishes
Or perhaps a memory
Just having someone to listen
It is what we all need

I've thought about that day
For many many years
I needed to tell the story
Though it may sound
completely weird

Because it isn't just a story
Of a girl and an indented screen
It's a story of survival
It's about being a human being

There's always someone to listen
And there's someone too who
cares
Just take that step to speak
your mind
Even if it's to a mirror

I hope I've given a voice
To all those who need to speak
But when I walk my dog in the
courtyard
I still see the dented screens

Sedona

No laughter for years
Now tears rolling down the
cheek
First time in a long time
You were truly free

Blessings will come along
When you're centered to the core
It may be a familiar feeling
That you've been right here
before

An open mind can see
And an open heart believes
A path to being truly happy
The road called opportunity

On your door she knocks
If you hesitate you lose
Put your hand upon the knob
Then you have to choose

Turn it or let it go
If you don't you'll never know
A future that's brought to
your door
Or a past that's just once more

Instead of a place of fear
Butterflies as your guide
Don't just run away
There's tranquility inside

She saw you standing there
With those bright healing eyes
A Sedona red rock view
And a babbling creek behind

A calming nature about you
A being of pure love
You began to speak
As though destined from above

Let nature be your guide
You were meant to meet
Don't over analyze
Just let it be

Thinking things through
Takes the energy away
Allow the whales song
If even for a day

If it goes anywhere
Nothing's just by chance
A passing spirit guide
Or a budding romance

Know this happiness
Exuding through your pores
You're good and deserving
To feel love once more

And what becomes of it
May be more complex
But you'll always have the
memory
Of the day at the Vortex

Sedona 2018

Dad had a concern
That we wouldn't get along
But we're all adults now
And he couldn't have been more wrong

From the first day
We all laughed so hard
Her head up in the wind
Our singing in the car

From the mustache cups
And the spilling of their wine
Brought about much laughter
And a hell of a good time

Baring ones soul
Tears rolling down our cheeks
We knew each other's feelings
We didn't have to speak

It was so enlightening
Not just the beauty all around
But what was deep inside
In each other's heart we found

The red rock mountain view
And the trails that we hiked
A sense of higher meaning
The timing was just right

We will always be together
No matter what life brings
We'll always have Sedona
And all its memories

Pain & Faith

What's the purpose
of this pain Lord
I cannot hear Your reply
I struggle for just a single word
Or see a sign from in the sky

Are You too sad that
You can't speak
Or show me what it's all about
Let me know why I'm torn apart
And why a new angel
sits on a cloud

Is there something
I should know
Am I to do life a little different
Is there anything to
everlasting life
Isn't that why Your Son was sent

But I am not able to visualize
And I just feel all alone
The world's darker now
than yesterday
When the last time the
brightness shone

I glance up and look
for the light
But I see the darkened sky
With some clouds
here and there
Every question I have
begins with why

Why don't You answer
The questions I ask
Have You ever answered me
It's hard to keep track

Why don't You lift this pain Lord
Do I have to have a special code
Am I going to find a
man behind a curtain
When I reach the
end of the road

When I don't hear a word
I wonder why You left
Or that You don't care
But maybe that You're deaf

Questioning Your motives
Is the devils bait
Since I may not get an answer
I just have to have faith

Personal Prison

I'm trapped in a cage
Please help me
I've been here so long
I just want to be free

My hands on the bars
I've no way out
I wonder what this captivity
Is all about

Once having autonomy
And the freedom to roam
Then I found myself taken
From my home

This place where I'm at
Is just so foreign
I search for answers
And strength within

I call on my senses
To get me out
But all I find is
Insecurity, fear, and doubt

No freedom for me
No lock to pick
No door to walk out
I decide to quit

Someone watching from
outside
Would plainly see
I brought about my own
Captivity

Why do I do this
To myself
If I'd just be honest
About how I felt

At times I may need help
As I travel through life
Let go of the bars I create
And walk through and fight

Give myself permission
To finally be free
No more mental prison
I can finally breathe

Perseverance

Perseverance in troubled times
Is it just a state of mind
Trying to locate the road to
peace
Though I search I cannot find

Issues behind they still haunt
And those ahead cause fear
The present allows me to
breathe
But anticipation brings on tears

Standing still is not an option
But there's no drive for
moving on
Climbing mountains over
and over
The will to live is all but gone

Taking a walk around tomorrow
Wondering where the road
will go
I find I've been walking in circles
What doesn't kill you helps
you grow

Down the manhole of life I fall
again
It seems someone keeps
moving the lids
Perhaps I should have taken
another path
But would it have made any
difference

So I follow where the sewer leads
Through sludge and lots of muck
I stop when I come to a fork in
the pipes
Left or right it's all just luck

Choosing which way I go
Will undoubtedly bring change
Do we control our destiny
Or is it pre-arranged

I just want to throw caution to
the wind
And see what happens next
Because analyzing everything
Just leaves me more perplexed

I think that I've found my
road sign
Not to peace but reality instead
Expect delays and left lane
closed
For construction and bumps
ahead

So I guess it really does matter
Which road you choose to take
After all He leads us wisely
If we're open to His pathways

Suicide Bliss

I'm withering away inside
Though I may be a light to you

Each day is a struggle
And so hard to get through

Life is not a challenge
For me it's a painful plight

I can't escape the torment
Though every day I try

Existence takes all my energy
And I feel so much despair

At times I can't get out of bed
And some days I just don't care

But I don't show you how I feel
You just see what I portray

Though there's no life in my eyes
And my soul is on its way

I let you see contentment
While I really feel confused

I still go through the motions
And laugh along with you

I may not isolate
And at times I may have fun

But inside I am dying
And I just want to be done

My thoughts have now gone
dark
And away from life I run

As I suffer alone in silence
And I don't tell anyone

What I used to see in color
Now I see in black and white

I close my eyes and I'm
comforted
I see the end in sight

I can't explain the bliss I feel
As I no longer have to fight

No longer numb with apathy
I can finally see the light

Suicide is not glamorous. It hurts. It hurts and affects everyone you know and even those you don't know. The thought of suicide or dying or taking your own life may seem like the answer, may seem like relief, may even seem like a welcome alternative to whatever is going on or what you are feeling or going through. The thing is, most of the time choosing life instead will eventually bring about a change or shift or another answer that you will be comfortable with. And, perhaps, your sticking around is to benefit or help someone else, albeit difficult to see this at the time. Life is not always about you but what you bring to someone else, maybe someone you don't even know right now. Trust in this thing called life. It's been around for a very long time and our very nature wants us to live. Sure it may seem "easier" to submit to suicide then to continue with what the issue, problem, or feeling is. But if you fight and continue to fight and even fight again and again, and then fight some more, although you may be absolutely and completely exhausted there will be a shift. Perhaps this shift will not be immediately known to you and will be instead for someone else. But stay open to the workings of the universe and eventually you may see the beauty and goodness that you bring by choosing life.

Suicide wants you. Suicide uses you. Suicide controls you. Suicide tricks you. Suicide convinces you of things that are not so. Suicide wants to win. Period. Don't let it win! DO NOT LET IT WIN!

If you are feeling suicidal or sad or depressed or fearful or destined or defeated or desperate or like you are being called by it or feel like it's an answer or you just want to end it, tell someone, call a hotline, call the suicide hotline at **1-800-273-8255**, call a hospital, call 911 or text CONNECT to 741741 from anywhere in the USA, anytime, about any type of crisis.

Speak up. Do not suffer in silence. You are not alone. YOU ARE NOT ALONE. JUST DON'T DO IT. SURVIVE WHATEVER THE ADVERSITY IS. NO MATTER WHAT DO NOT GIVE UP. DO NOT GIVE IN. FIGHT!

My Zen

I sought out to search for my zen
To find the lost path inside
I don't know when the myopia began
But like a turtle my head I'd hide

Where to go on a conscious level
But more than that inner misdirection
Going against the ego's gavel
I brought light to all the destruction

I found the corner of lost and revenge
While in the belly of the sewer
The path that led me right to zen
A place of peace seen by the viewer

The place not found when quick to anger
It seems anything worthwhile takes a fight
Sit crossed legged thumb and forefinger
Say a mantra time after time

Become centered on not a thing
Let the energy pierce your doubting skin
Soon you'll find that this will bring
Peace and strength to begin again

Find yourself and who you are
And leave behind all the drama
Zen is being centered where you are
Within the confines of asana

I think it's just being comfortable
Where you are and where you've been
The key to staying mindful now
Is when you're able to find your zen

Mental Holocaust

My mind is like a holocaust
My inner compass has been lost
I feel the pain of the suffering
And the anguish that
their death brings

Empathy for the innocent
So much mental torment
The searing of the
knife in the side
Like a branding it's in my mind

With a twist, it's all
puppies and rainbows
Nobody, not even me knows
I continue on seeing
the trees, fish, sky
Never aware to ask why

Then it comes to me each night
All the chaos and I realize
The boogey man
underneath my bed
Is really here in my head

It comes and goes
at its own will
But when it's gone I feel it still
Like all the victims sick or killed
I have no wall upon
which to build

For so long I tried to hide
And keep the sorrow
deep inside
Slow at first then waves begun
Teary eyed no place to run

It seems there's nothing
else but fate
Leaving behind sadness,
pain, and hate
One road stops another begins
Til the day the chaos ends

Up above imagined peace
Where illness and fighting cease
The sun rises then it sets
The tormented mind
can finally rest

Miracles

At times it looks like
Fate intervenes
As things come together
A random happening

Long lost sisters
Living next door
They just thought
They were only neighbors

He gave a kidney
To a stranger
To find out later
It was his brother

Many experiences
That can't be explained away
Some call it the universe
Others say it's fate

Whatever it is
Happens on a daily basis
It can't just be random
There's so many cases

Call it what you want
Maybe even magical
What if they were
Really miracles

Miracles performed
From Heaven above
All He wants for us
Is a sharing of love

But we don't think of them
As miracles at all
That would frighten us
So we build up a wall

Imagine what it could be like
If we all just believed
Let down our guard
And enjoy what He creates

No More Pain

Seeing the sky from both sides
I've seen the dark I've seen the
light
Oh how I wish I could see again
That that made me way
back when

Back when young with no real
cares
Except at night when I was
scared
But that would end with passing
seasons
And I learned there really was a
reason

I put my foot down to maturity
A child I wanted to remain
you see
Curl up in a ball and cry out
my eyes
Without ever really
knowing why

With age came responsibility
And caring too much with
empathy
I ached for those who were
in pain
So much so it began to drive
me insane

Showing a smile throughout the
days
I didn't know any other way
I just wanted others to think I
was fine
When inside I think I had
already died

The day He took my friend
from me
I realized that I didn't need
Anyone to hold my hand again
For I knew how the story
would end

Now above the clouds I see it all
And on your phone I'd like to call
You just have to believe I'm
watching you
From way up high with an
awesome view

I hold out my hands and
comfort souls
Whether the very young or the
very old
Now I know why I had to do
my time
I had to walk in their shoes to
make it right

No more pain from where I sit
No more wondering and no
regrets
Just helping others to get by
So they can live a happy life

No more pain from where I sit
No more wondering and no
regrets
Just helping others to get by
So they can live a happy life

Suicide is not glamorous. It hurts. It hurts and affects everyone you know and even those you don't know. The thought of suicide or dying or taking your own life may seem like the answer, may seem like relief, may even seem like a welcome alternative to whatever is going on or what you are feeling or going through. The thing is, most of the time choosing life instead will eventually bring about a change or shift or another answer that you will be comfortable with. And, perhaps, your sticking around is to benefit or help someone else, albeit difficult to see this at the time. Life is not always about you but what you bring to someone else, maybe someone you don't even know right now. Trust in this thing called life. It's been around for a very long time and our very nature wants us to live. Sure it may seem "easier" to submit to suicide then to continue with what the issue, problem, or feeling is. But if you fight and continue to fight and even fight again and again, and then fight some more, although you may be absolutely and completely exhausted there will be a shift. Perhaps this shift will not be immediately known to you and will be instead for someone else. But stay open to the workings of the universe and eventually you may see the beauty and goodness that you bring by choosing life.

Suicide wants you. Suicide uses you. Suicide controls you. Suicide tricks you. Suicide convinces you of things that are not so. Suicide wants to win. Period. Don't let it win! DO NOT LET IT WIN!

If you are feeling suicidal or sad or depressed or fearful or destined or defeated or desperate or like you are being called by it or feel like it's an answer or you just want to end it, tell someone, call a hotline, call the suicide hotline at **1-800-273-8255**, call a hospital, call 911 or text CONNECT to 741741 from anywhere in the USA, anytime, about any type of crisis.

Speak up. Do not suffer in silence. You are not alone. YOU ARE NOT ALONE. JUST DON'T DO IT. SURVIVE WHATEVER THE ADVERSITY IS. NO MATTER WHAT DO NOT GIVE UP. DO NOT GIVE IN. FIGHT!

My Oz

When I look behind the curtain
Who is it that I find
Is Oz really just parts of me
Deceptions of my mind

Does the curtain and the drama
Keep me safe from who I am
Defenses all in place
Personal truth be damned

Concealed discomforts
from myself
And I learned to hide from fear
Somehow I have to face it
Without the costume that I wear

Sometimes I feel too much
You may call it empathy
But when I feel with my heart
I call it anxiety

Without a feeling now
I'm like a tin robot
When I see others having fun
I feel like I've been robbed

At times my thoughts get lost
Like I have straw for a brain
Am I hiding from reality
Can I ever go home again

Along the colored bricks
I take a little stroll
And look deep within myself
Before deception takes its toll

Defense mechanisms in check
Breaking down my minds wall
Lubing the rusty
corners of my eyes
I realize I'm whole after all

Now when I pull
back the curtain
I'm not afraid to see
The one who stood
there shaking
Was just a part of me

Hey Mister

Hey mister
Man in the moon
Can you come out
And play

I've been good
I went to school
I've been waiting
For you all day

Hey mister
Man in the moon
Can you play
Til this day ends

I'm awful lonely
By myself
And I have
No friends

Hey mister
Man in the moon
Do you ever
Talk

Maybe if you
Climb down here
We could go
For a walk

Hey mister
Man in the moon
Can you
Tie my shoe

My brother said
You're made of cheese
And sometimes
You turn blue

Hey mister
Man in the moon
Can you be
My friend

We could play
Lots of games
I'll even
Let you win

Hey mister
Man in the moon
Can you stay
With me at night

I'm afraid
To go to sleep
Daddy says
The bed bugs bite

Hey mister
Man in the moon
We could play
Hide-n-seek

I can be it
I'll count to ten
I promise
I won't peek

Hey mister
Man in the moon
Do you want
To play cards

We could play
Go fish
I could teach you
It's not hard

Hey mister
Man in the moon
Will you sit
With me

This one's yours
This one's mine
We'll have
A tea party

Hey mister
Man in the moon
Can you read me
Charlotte's Web

I'll let you turn
The pages
Then I will go
To bed

Hey mister
Man in the moon
We could climb
A tree

We need to go
Really high
So lava won't
Get me

Hey mister
Man in the moon
Can you fix
My bear

He looks like
My mommy
He doesn't have
Any hair

Hey mister
Man in the moon
Can we sing
A song

Mommy used to
Sing with me
Now she sleeps
All day long

Hey mister
Man in the moon
Can you make
Mommy better

We used to play
All the time
And I really really
Love her

Hey mister
Man in the moon
Can you go with me
To school

If you did
The other kids
Would think
I'm very cool

Lost at Sea

I breathe but there's no air
I talk but there are no words
I see but there's no color
I listen but do not hear

I seek to feel but I am numb
I walk but I'm paralyzed
I can't blow the wind
into my sails
My boat is about to capsize

I try to laugh but I
can't even smile
I want to believe but
there's only fear
Though there's enough
to fill the ocean
I want to cry but there
are no tears

Like a ship taking on water
In the middle of a hurricane
There's no help to be found
Though I call for a mayday

Do I go down with the ship
Do I steer into the waves
Do I still have the strength
To face another day

I pray 'ship don't pass me by'
As I try to get in a life boat
Though I think I cannot act
I try to dream but have no hope

When the storm has
finally passed
And I've been thrust
upon the rocks
I wonder if I'll ever be found
Or if perhaps I've
never been lost

My Dementia

I'm older now
And lost to a forgetful mind
I search for the past
But the memories I cannot find

It's like the brain can
no longer see
Or like a wave you cannot ride
It's like a fishbowl fish
without a life
Or building sandcastles
too close to the tide

I see someone or something
That sparks a thought
I try to remember
Then the thought is lost

Forgetting faces of family
Not knowing who are friends
Does one with dementia
even know
To want the forgetfulness
to end

It steals ones freedom
It steals ones thoughts
Suddenly forgetting everything
That I had been taught

I know the sanity won't last
And the clarity will get less clear
I know my memory
will get worse
Being left alone is what I fear

And family and friends
Repeat many times
Because I forget
What I left behind

I know the time will
come someday
This fear creates anxiety
I know I'll be put away
When no one can
take care of me

My mind is gone
But my shell remains
It's like hide-n-seek
But this is no game

So I count to ten
No one I see
Locked within
Olly olly oxen free

Lifecycle of Trees

They used the wood
from the gallows
To support Him while He said
Take this cup from me if You will
Before I end up dead

But all the time He really knew
That that's why He came to be
To save a few or save the world
The good, the bad, you, and me

Even the flowers of
the redbud tree
Did atone for its role
But not when one
chooses to escape
By utilizing the gallows pole

Is it atonement or escape
It depends on the
story being told
Is one running to or
running from
Or it the selling of ones soul

The power of the dogwood tree
No longer capable
of being a cross
Its height forever
dwarfed in size
Its initial role forever lost

Beauty, sturdiness,
or how it's used
Determines how a tree's defined
Providing shade or food to eat
Even manchineel can
make you blind

The tree of life is no longer true
Its thorns man made
into a crown
Man manipulates its innocence
But euphorbia still
blooms year round

Purpose changes as
life moves along
It doesn't always end
how it sets out
Man intervenes and the
road gets blocked
Fate's no longer what
it's all about

Farmer

I'm only here on earth
Because of my ancestors
I'm very proud of them
As they were farmers

They always got up early
And worked very long days
Though muscles had to be
hurting
They never complained

No matter what food they raised
Allowed me to have a plate full
And for their personal sacrifices
I will be forever grateful

Sometimes you never know
Who you affect down the line
Though there may be adversity
And you go through difficult
times

You have had a very
thankless job
But I appreciate what you
still do
And for that I want to say
A very big thank you!

Land may be getting more scarce
And that could be causing
you fear
Take a break and find yourself
Because without you I wouldn't
be here

As you ponder your future
And wake before the rising sun
I pray that you continue
To feed the world one by one

I thank you for
The food that I eat
My daily bread
And the milk that I drink

I thank you for
The food you provide
You've been helping mankind
From the beginning of time

I thank you for
All the work that you do
Up daily before dawn
And when you're sick too

Most people on earth
Don't have a clue
But you're the reason we're here
That is so very true

With so little rest
Working day and night
Thank you always
For sustaining my life

My Demons

My demons are never
Going to go away
I'll have a good moment
Then several bad days

The demons are numerous
And they always come back
Maybe it's a different demon
But torment they do not lack

I'm so tired of waiting
Cuz I know something's
gonna happen
People are so stupid
The demons obviously
have them

Too tired to go on
Just more shit on a different day
The details may be different
But the demons end
game is the same

Well screw it I'm tired
I don't care where I end up
Cuz it didn't pass me by
The proverbial stupid cup

A deep breath I take
And inhale more gas
Maybe now it'll end
All the bullshit at last

Goodbye damn demons
And those I love too
I have to go now
I'm way overdue

Perhaps I'll finally find the peace
That I've searched for for years
It'll come at a cost
The cost of the tears

A black hole on the road of life
I see it but still fall
History becomes altered
Once and for all

Kintsugi Strong

The darkness dawns
And stays at dusk
Through the night
Tears turn to rust

You feel you're cracked
Your hope's been sold
But Kintsugi potters
Fill cracks with gold

The final product
Is stronger still
Like deep inside
Hides your will

The clay is stronger
With imperfection
Through the cracks there's light
We learn a lesson

You may feel broken
Like cracked pottery
It makes you more resilient
Adversity

Kintsugi - Japanese art of filling pottery or china cracks with gold
In other words, we're all cracked but
those cracks make us stronger.
Through the cracks there's light

Life (A Metaphor)

The forest is thick
With trees and fog
Trying to find my way out
I become more lost

It'll take courage
Strength and will
To get beyond
That mammoth hill

Sometimes it's hard
When hiking alone
Which way to turn
Which way to go

Up I climb
But down I fall
I get up slowly
And begin to crawl

With nothing left
I sit and wonder
All of a sudden
It begins to thunder

The rain comes down
I'm soaked to the bone
Why am I here
I just wanna go home

I find a cave
And wait out the storm
Lost in this world
From the day I was born

My compass is broken
Please show me the way
With no other option
I begin to pray

I'm lost and confused
In the dark all alone
Let your Light shine
And guide me home

I've been here before
Baggage dragging behind
But when in the forest
It'll make you blind

The darkness comes
So you can see the light
He's always there
Like the stars in the sky

Overwhelming indeed
Pull the curtain aside
And face your fears
Don't run and hide

I must let go
Of what's weighing me down
And holding me back
It's time to move on

Take that first step
It's all in the mind
The clearing's ahead
One breath at a time

Loyal Friend

When the sun rises
A new day begins
Possibilities are endless
When you have a loyal friend

If you get into trouble
A friend stands by your side
In times of darkness
They can be a bright light

One to share your thoughts with
And lend a helpful ear
One to get you through it
When there's times of fear

When life gets you down
And you're asking why
A friend will hold you up
And help you fight the fight

If you cry a tear
And it rolls down your cheek
A friend will hand you tissue
Not think that you are weak

The friends of the friendless
Will always be around
And when you're feeling lost
They'll stay until you're found

From A Patient's Perspective

I lay here tired and in pain
With no privacy and
staring at the ceiling
I can't even think for myself
And not being home
is a lonely feeling

The staff comes in and
out waking me
When I just fall asleep
Poking and prodding
til I'm tapped out
I smile though I want to weep

I count the holes in
the ceiling tiles
And see imperfections
on the walls
I'm left exposed with
my ass hanging out
And no one answers when I call

I'm at your mercy day and night
I didn't ask to be hurt or ill
I just want to be whole again
And I can with your
help and skill

I know what I need
if you'll listen
Take a moment I'm people too
I can't always abide
by your schedule
Not that I'm an ungrateful fool

I appreciate your time
and attention
Though the words I
cannot speak
At one time I was
strong like you
Now I lay here
dependent and weak

I'm grateful for your
encouragement
And I'm glad for the
care you're giving
I just want to be
comfortable again
And deal with this new
life I've been given

Just try to take a
little more time
In your day when caring for me
Laying here is not what I want
So please don't judge
or ignore my needs

Treat me with dignity
and respect
And don't give up if I
start slipping away
With your help and empathy
I'm sure to get better every day

Drinking and Driving (A Dedication to Carl)

I was minding my own business
Taking a stroll one night
When you went out drinking
And decided to drive

I was thinking how tomorrow
I'd get up and go to church
But then you hit me with
your car
And left me in a ditch hurt

I couldn't feel the pain
Or even move a muscle
When I woke up and was
paralyzed
In a local hospital

You never slowed you never
stopped
You went on about your way
Did you even know you hit
someone
When you woke up the
next day

For months I lay in a
hospital bed
Just fighting to survive
But I often thought of you
And how you got on with
your life

I felt nothing from my neck down
I couldn't even move a limb
Unlike you I'd never be able
To feed or dress myself again

Thank goodness for my family
Who kept me clean and neat
And because you drove drunk
that night
I will always have a seat

A wheelchair for life
Was the sentence I received
While you just went back to
the bar
Not caught and so relieved

Many demons came along
The night of the accident
Til the day I took a gun
And decided to end it

You see that night you drove
drunk
You really took my life
But before that you made sure
My life was full of strife

I wonder as I sit here
On a cloud up in the sky
Why that night you decided
That you would drink and drive

And then after you hit me
Did you ever give a damn
Was your life even altered
And would you do it all again

One day karma will pay you back
And deliver your final fate
Cuz for nearly forty years
I paid for your mistake

Don't Let The Darkness Win

He left me
On my darkest day
I'm all alone
At least I feel that way

Mental torment
And a home that was torn
Life's been total chaos
From the day I was born

It's been such a struggle
Out loud I cried
"God why did You abandon me?
I'm dead inside"

The pain's too much
I have no hope
It'll never change
I grab the rope

Up on the chair
Noose over head
It's too late now
I take a step

As I do
Everything goes black
Too late now
I can't go back

But before I stepped
One more round
I prayed to God
I'm not hell bound

I asked for forgiveness
My last task
In a voice He said
"I forgive those who ask"

Life may be very scary and you may think there's no other way. Hope can come spontaneously. There may be a mental shift in ways that you do not yet know. Give every day a chance and don't give up no matter what, no matter how dark or painful it gets. As long as you are able to breathe, reach out and keep on reaching out. Become willing to be vulnerable, to change, to take a chance. Scary, yes, but you are not alone. Ever. If you are feeling suicidal please call 911, a hospital, or the National Suicide Hotline at **1-800-273-8255 or text CONNECT to 741741**

Borderline

When my mind races
I get lost
Incessant worrying
And constant thoughts

Like a tickle inside
The anxiety kills
Focus on breathing
But I feel it still

Sadness looms
I don't know why
A deep dark place
I run and hide

A change in mood
Maybe this times the last
But it's not
Up and down so fast

I love you I hate you
Which one today
The rage is strong
Get out of my way

Black and white
No shades of grey
I'll hurt myself
If you don't stay

Drinking or drugs
Quiet the torment inside
Fear abates
Where abandonment resides

Maintain control
For stability
Manipulation
Watch me bleed

Unbeknownst to me
My mind provides
What I need to be freed
Come hell or high tide

Blaming others
I must always be right
Loneliness continues
With no insight

I just hate who I am
Down deep in my bones
Acceptance is key
But I remain all alone

When you're not okay
With feeling fine
You've just crossed over
The borderline

You don't choose
The way you are
Time can change things
But it will be hard

We're all dealt something
The battles in life
You have strength inside you
To fight the fight

Accept life's plan
And the road you're on
That's the first step
A new day will dawn

Dis-ease

I don't understand
Why I have this disease
It seems like You
Have abandoned me

Why have You given me
This cross to bear
Is it because
You need me near

The pain and dysfunction
Is so hard on me
And on those watching
Like friends and family

I see myself
Withering away
A little bit worse
Everyday

I pray for a miracle
For You to perform
Was this the reason
I was born

Does this have
Little to do with me
Or more for others
As they watch and see

Is it to change
Their life not mine
Is it so
Purpose they find

I guess I don't mind
The suffering
If for someone's benefit
It can eventually bring

But in the meantime
From this I want to run
That's probably because
I'm just human

Even your Son asked that
The cup pass Him by
Is this disease
The purpose of my life

I've finally realized
My Godly fate
Take me Home
I don't want to be late

I've been used as a vessel
To get a message through
To many people
Or maybe a few

Learn from my illness
What you need to get by
I'm now in a better place
No need to cry

Dig In

When the world's so cruel
And you just want it to end
And you want to scream
That's when you need to dig in

Dig in hard
And do what you can
Don't give up
Formulate a plan

A plan for surviving
The cruelty of it all
Get your feelings out
And don't build a wall

When it seems
People are all bad
And the whole world
Is going mad

Remember it's just temporary
What you're feeling
at the moment
Being angry and jaded
Can be a lethal component

Take a breath
And remember some good
When you felt lighter
And kindness stood

It can be overwhelming
The challenges of this life
But others will stand with you
When you stand up
for what's right

Rise above the adversity
When it's difficult to cope
Don't go through it alone
And don't give up hope

It might even help
If you're one who believes
Just ask for strength
To find serenity

Darkness Is Not Always Dark

A rock may have no lifecycle
Its' purpose just to 'be'
And we may not be able to
understand
With our limited ability

Though there may be affliction
It's not a punishment
And a world in chaos
It may not make any sense

Disappointment or misfortune
May not be all about you
But perhaps another's
observations
Of the things that you do

Suffering and pain
Though not equal or fair
Sometimes injustice
Is the cross you must bear

Perhaps you're living with
adversity
But for some reason you're
where you are
Words can't really heal a wound
On some level there's still a scar

Either physically or mentally
There's some kind of memory
Whether or not it's consciously
seen
Perhaps to heal is spirituality

Belief brings solace when
feeling lonely
Having faith in Him gives hope
Dig down deep for strength
When pushed to the end of
your rope

You can forget or choose to
ignore
So there's no suffering or pain
It's difficult in the midst of a
challenge
But hit reset again

Take things a day at a time
But if that's too overwhelming
Take things one breath at a time
Focus, and keep going

I know that it's not easy
But there's no chance of things
improving
Life can't get any better
Once you have stopped
breathing

Never lose hope and never
give up
Although 'Never,' in itself brings
fright
Only in darkness do you see the
stars
But they're always there in the
light

Just because you can't see it
Doesn't mean that it's not there
There's hope beyond what
we know
And 'Science' can only take us
so far

California Hotel

I stayed at the California hotel
On a vacation of sorts
But there was a tremendous
storm
So I decided to head to
another port

I went to the hotels' front desk
He asked me what I was here
about
I handed him my room key
Cuz I was checking out

He looked at me puzzled
He must have seen I was in
pieces
He asked me sincerely
Are you ready to leave us

I answered him softly
Please figure up my bill
While he did so
The memories came back still

There were so many good ones
But outside there's so much hate
With a tear in my eye
I signed my name and paid

By the time I reached the door
I realized the path
And once I stepped foot on it
There'd be no going back

The doorman said good day
ma'am
I thought 'if it only were'
I've already checked out
And I'll be leaving here for sure

It suddenly dawned on me
Why I chose to stay at the
California hotel
It was a time of sadness
T'which upon my knees I fell

Now it's just the opposite
There's sunshine on my face
Happy to be on my way
And out of this horrible place

I thought of all the craziness
When life is such a gift
I had to get a move on
If I wanted to catch the ship

Once at the marina
I glanced back once more
Here's to the future
Then I climbed aboard

Cruel god

Why are you so cruel
To the ones that I love
Are you that superior
Sitting high up above

Are we just your play-doh
To be molded then put away
Are we just your play toys
That you take out every day

Do you like to see our pain
So we fall onto our knees
Promising you the world
And pretending to believe

We ask you for one more thing
And expect you to perform
A simple little miracle
Like the day that we were born

We're often hit when we're
already down
So what's the point of that
Do we need to go outside
And have a little chat

Why don't you just show
your face
Are you so little of a man
Why hide behind the curtain
You talk bigger than you stand

You're the one with the fear
That's why you use power
Otherwise you'd run away
And in a corner you'd cower

So let's just put it out there
You're no more god than me
You just have the know-how
To make the heavens, earth,
and sea

I know all of this hurts you too
Though you allow suffering
and pain
Because when you're upset
You cause it to really rain

Can we compromise
To stop the pain and hurt
So we can live in harmony
Before this gets any worse

Let's just call a truce
Please have a little heart
Don't take my toys way
from me
Then we can have a brand new
start

Mom

For as long as I remember
You've been taking care of me
So long I never thought
You would ever leave

Family always first
Faith through and through
Always taking care of others
Making sure that they had food

Vicks on the chest when sick
You kept me warm
when I was cold
You even warmed
socks by the oven
When did you start to get old

You'd lay down your life for me
Protect me at all costs
Give me all I needed
Find me when I was lost

As you started to fade away
Loose ends needed to be tied
It's hard to say when it started
The daily tears and
the asking why

Every week more forgetful
Than the week before
What I'd give for one more day
To talk with you once more

The you we had come to know
The dementia slowly took away
Though the love was fierce
We knew you couldn't stay

It seems like overnight
Your eyes no longer
showed your soul
Though your shell
remained behind
You grew the wings of an angel

We shared a birthday every year
And we had that special bond
You were my best friend
I'll always love you Mom

You

You take from me
What's important and true
My mind and body
Turned over to you

When you're around
You strangle me
Mentally and physically
I cannot breathe

You're so powerful
My every thought and move
Is under your control
I don't argue

For if I do
You only get worse
And hit me again
You I curse

When I think you're gone
You reappear
Sending me reeling
I fall with fear

There is nothing
That I can do
Try as I may
To get rid of you

You make me feel
So unsure
You steal my confidence
Now I'm insecure

You take away
My feeling of safety
My sense of calm
And my ability

You make me doubt
Who I am
I don't even know
Who I've become

I shutter and shake
When you're around
And when you're not
My heart still pounds

I isolate
In bed I stay
And on myself
I put the blame

Inside and out
You control me
A powerful feeling
'You' are – Anxiety

An Open Mind
Can See

When you believe
There's more in the air than
just wind
Then you start thinking about
things
Over and over again

If darkness
Travels faster than light
Then at times of total darkness
Is when you have to fight

If the yellow brick road
Leads you to Oz
Then pull back the curtain
And take a long pause

If all the stars
Align in the sky
Do you accept it
Or do you ask why

If it is what you make it
How do you know which way is
right
One way can bring fortune
And the other plight

We're all left with choices
And decisions to make
Close your eyes and seek
guidance
To help uncertainty abate

Sometimes adversity
Strikes again and again
But it allows opportunity
For you to begin

When one chapter ends
Think of it as a star burst
One had to end
To form the universe

He filled the world
With everything you need
Just open your mind
To see the possibilities

Existence came together
In sequence and time
For you at this moment
Keep that in mind

Addiction

It captivated you
From the beginning
With total euphoria
It kept your head spinning

Winning is what
You always tried for
But you couldn't stop
Even when dirt poor

The rush of excitement
When you'd win a hand
Roulette, slots
Craps or blackjack

You couldn't quit
No matter the pain
As you hurt your family
Again and again

You would try for the high
You once knew
But you'd need more
As your tolerance grew

You needed more and more
It was always on your mind
You became someone else
And you weren't kind

Your drug of choice took
precedence
Over all aspects of your life
Everything else took a back seat
You couldn't stop if you tried

You also got into trouble
And you missed a lot of work
The list keeps on growing
Of the people that you hurt

It's your demon
Drugs and drinking
Nicotine and porn
Sex and gambling

Whatever the addiction
It's always the same
Chasing the high
Somewhat of a game

It's got the control
You have none
You just know
You gotta do it again

Take a look at yourself
Take a good look
You didn't set out
To get hooked

But you've become
Someone so lost
With the demon a part of you
It's such a high cost

It hurts so much
The anxiety and pain
When you try to stop
So you do it again

But stopping begins
When you refuse to get high
With the demons behind you
You'll learn to get by

Stopping is hard
No need to do it by yourself
Just speak up and allow
Others to help

Giving it up
Won't be a breeze
It'll takes lots of work
And won't be easy

When you start kicking
It'll be rough
But you can get through it
It's time to hang tough

Stay in the now
Minute to minute
Take it a breath at a time
You're in it to win it

Keep telling yourself
Again and again
You'll get a life back
The demons won't win

Abuse

I still hear the sound of his car
Pulling into the drive
The sound of the front
door opening
And the fear I felt inside

I'd hold my breath hoping
He'll leave me alone today
But no such luck he's
already drunk
I try to get out of his way

I remember the sound
of his footsteps
As I'd hide and try to
think of a plan
But as soon as he found
me he'd hit me
More than once with
the back of his hand

At other times he'd molest me
Or hit me with his belt
I'd leave my body and mentally
I'd have to go somewhere else

I thought that it was over
The day he left my mom
My scars started to heal
Then another came along

Sometimes I'd let him hurt me
So my siblings could get away
I'd rather take the abuse
For the others to be safe

For years I felt so dirty
Maybe I could have fought
But their words were so hurtful
And I believed that
it was my fault

The memories burned
like a candle
In my mind I blamed myself
Until I told my story
And I got a lot of help

Kids should not have to pay
For someone who's
so deranged
Know that it was not your fault
And others feel your pain

Abuser

Sometimes I run to a place
A doorway that I go through
Even if just mentally
To get away from you

When I hear the footsteps
It is you that I fear
Once you'd been so kind
So many faces that you wear

You can be good and fun
To everybody else
But how many more children
Are victims like myself

You first conned me
With your 'special' way
And you didn't stop
With me you'd want to play

From that day on
I was made to feel
No trusting anyone else
What the hell was your deal

I couldn't speak up
When I was young you
threatened me
My dreams were always haunted
When I saw you in my sleep

You had no right to abuse me
You are a sick one
I couldn't fight you off
I was way too young

But now I am older
And you are just plain old
I'm no longer quiet
My story I have told

I wish that I had told someone
When I was a little kid
Then I wouldn't have had to
Run away and hid

But that was in the past
When I wanted to be dead
Now I'm working through it
I'm living life instead

You can no longer hurt me
Because now I'm being heard
Though maybe not in this life
You'll still get what you deserve

I hold that child close
The one that once was me
We will never be alone again
Now that we are free

Alcoholic

When you started drinking
You didn't have a care
Then it became more frequent
And went downhill from there

You became an alcoholic
And hurt your family
Generations later
It finally got to me

Though I did get through it
It surely wasn't fun
It's strange how this all starts
With "I'll think I'll have just one"

Remember when you held
my hand
Over the candle flame
I didn't argue or talk back
You still did it again

You became so cruel and mean
To others you were nice
Depending if you were drinking
Sober, you saved a life

You lost your self-respect
And lots of money too
The sadness is you don't realize
I was once so proud of you

Through the many, many years
No one has been spared
We've all seen the damage done
And it cannot be repaired

Though I'm through
enabling you
If you want to turn things
around
I will be there for you
When you're AA bound

Perhaps genetics played a part
But you have the ability
To start over here and now
And find serenity

It's affected so many
Family members through the
years
It is called a disease
And it cannot be cured

Although it can be treated
One must admit just one line
"I am an alcoholic"
Take it a day at a time

8 X 10

Life is not an 8 X 10
It's like a river always moving
Having challenges and dams
Sometimes never ending

It's like red rock mountains
from wind and rain
The structure's always changing
Guaranteed ups and downs
A path that's always winding

Life may not be an 8 x 10
But at times it needs to be
Remembering a time
less stressed
A time to stop and see

What do you want from this life
Perhaps time will tell
But with direction and a plan
You can have it all

All you want and all you need
Is already here on earth
It's been here since
the beginning
But you must be centered first

Like sand through your fingers
Time is not an 8 X 10
A fearless step towards
the future
Instead of being stuck
where you've been

When your candle's burning low
Remember it's nothing
more than wax
But a memory hanging
on your wall
Is something that will last

So along this road of life
Take photos once again
Endless possibilities
Life as an 8 X 10

Yesterday's Time

Sitting on the park bench
Waiting for a friend
Watching the birds
And the time go by

It's been a while
The age of innocence
Now living for someone else
Cuz my life's not mine

The wind picks up
And the sun starts to set
Where did it go
All of yesterday's time

Yesterday's time
Yesterday's time

Seems like the past
Is but a dream
Like it wasn't even real
Or just a figment of the mind

Kids wish to be older
Elder's wishes become few
Cuz there's less time in front
And way more behind

Why can't we see
What we need to
And why can't we believe
When something is true

The faster life goes
Spinning out of control
We're on a freeway
And not a dirt road

Yesterday's time
Yesterday's time

Take it for granted
Time will be there
But yesterday's gone
And tomorrow's not here

Waiting for no one
And suddenly realize
There's no borrowing
From yesterday's time

Yesterday's time
Yesterday's time

I Don't Remember When

I don't remember when
Life was ever fair
Or when in a crib
You pulled my hair

But I remember
The good times that we had
What made us happy
What made us sad

And I never intentionally
Brought harm to you
I still can't remember
Who choked out who

I didn't mean to hurt you
With a swing or on the scale
I would feel it too
When you stepped on a nail

We'd play with hot wheels
On a dirt track at the side
Our imaginations endless
Many a good time

And the cement smell
When they built the pool
And in the parking lot
The Cox airplane fuel

And in the daytime
I'd steal food to eat
Doritos in bed at night
Instead of sleep

We had favorite games
Like Green Ghost
Monopoly and Masterpiece
We had a haunted house

At the church field we'd play
Often until dusk
Or when Chester would come
Chasing after us

Statue maker and tag
Go fish and war
Stringing cans at night
Here comes a car

Hiding in the trees
Waiting for what comes
When we were kids
We had some fun

A spaceship outside
And army men
I was so lucky
You were my friend

But times got rough
Things just weren't fair
When we didn't talk
For a couple years

I was glad when
Finally we grew
And now we get to pull
Each other through

I cherish the memories
When we were tight
Though the games we played
Usually ended in a fight

Today as then
We were side by side
Like in our cowboy outfits
And Top Star we would ride

As adults now
More responsibility
Here's to Speed Racer
And Emergency!

Life is no longer
A game of hide-n-seek
When you want to give up
There's no olly olly oxen free

But if life presents a challenge
We face it together there's no
doubt
Maybe the hokey pokey
Is what it's all about

Tears when hurt or a game is lost
Realizing things aren't fair
But I guess that all started
From the time you pulled my hair

A Broken Wing

I was born
With tiny wings
They weren't much good
For anything

On the others
I relied
To teach me some
Of life's guidelines

There came a time
On the edge of the nest
I needed to venture out
With all the rest

This was the test
Of my ability
With confidence
I could be free

But I had
A broken wing
I knew alone
I couldn't do a thing

Was I not taught
What I needed to know
With one false step
I'd fall below

The broken wing
Was also due to me
For not doing my part
When I reached maturity

I was supposed to have taken
What I had learned
I can't blame others
For not being stern

One has to know
That it takes two
When a lesson's taught
Even in youth

Had I been more
Of a receptive being
I wouldn't have
A broken wing

So now I make
The best of it all
Before I walk
I learn to crawl

You All Know Who You Are

You tried to silence our words
And our virtuous ways
You called them dissertations
Why were you so afraid

Did you not take an oath
Did you not have good in your heart
Why didn't you respect others
Were you this way from the start

I heard you talk behind their backs
You are two-faced through and through
Why didn't you ever speak the truth
Were you afraid of what they'd do

You were like a poison
With infection spreading wide
With so many others under your spell
I had to bide my time

So many suffered needlessly
When you didn't listen to what was said
You didn't want us to be right
So several ended up dead

I wonder how you sleep at night
Considering all the harm you create
One day karma will bite your ass
And you will face the wrath of fate

But A Dream?

Life isn't always happy
Nor can we always cope
But things can only get better
When we have a little hope

Do the clouds ever disappear
Or do we just stop noticing
Does the music seem to stop
Or did we just stop singing

Are we really by ourselves
Perhaps wishing for a family
Do we get lost in a crowd
Or are we very lonely

Do we think others won't understand
Are we afraid that they'll taunt us
Do we just need to take care of ourselves
And not think about the stigma

Is all of life but a dream
A trick of the subconscious
Questioning was it real or not
Reality does haunt us

Two Sides

Slam the door
Punch the wall
Break a window
Destroy it all

Naive one
Watch and learn
Cuz someday
It'll be your turn

Is it personality
Or perhaps a bad day
Is it something more than that
I want to go out and play

There goes another dish
Iron flying through the air
The crash of a set of glasses
More than one can bear

Maybe I'll drive off a cliff
Or into a block wall
Am I really hearing this
Scared, I begin to ball

Don't forget your jackets
Or your boots outside there's rain
Is it safe, be careful hon
Begin to go insane

No one else is accepted
Just the three of us
How to have friends and
relationships
With a family that doesn't trust

Keep our family secrets
No matter how you feel
Silent treatment for talking back
Soap in mouth was real

Tension at the table
Go to bed without dinner
I hate you came outta my mouth
Don't you say another word

I wondered how many children
Go without love or food
And are only shown affection
Depending if they're good

The other side a loving heart
And caring that didn't quit
Brought about confusion
In my life and in my head

You went on as normal
When there were issues
through the years
A poor start in a loving home
The beginning of your fears

Today I see things differently
You did the best that you
could do
If you had had the insight
You would have changed a
thing or two

Now you're old and feeble
And have dementia too
I would like to be able to forget
The things you used to do

I'm grateful for the empathy
But there was damage done
However I've moved beyond it
And it doesn't define who I am

Run Away

It's easy to just run away
We learned that just about
everyday
It's much harder to stay
Even when going to the beach
to play

It didn't matter if it was fun or
exciting
Beginning was always cause for
anxiety
Enjoy the new toy- only if I could
Put off, or just don't, feel the good

Before the responsibilities came
We used to play so many games
Hide n seek, cans, and tag
Happiness and joy, then what
a drag

At the side, remnants of the
leaves we burned
Were we lucky about a lesson
learned?
Rapid change and sudden loss
Silent treatment and a bitter
frost

Out of the blue the rain came
down
Instead of boots, we wore a
frown
It didn't matter young or grown
Only time till we're disowned

It didn't matter a cliff or wall
I only knew to cringe and ball
In life it was but a pause
But nonetheless detrimental to
our cause

Now it's realized it was the best
they could
But the dash for me was all
but good
The hurt the pain its all the same
Old or young the fear remains

Life it can be so intense
Like checkers or a game of
chess
Anxiety to take a step
I don't think I was fully prepped

Fear, anxiety, a whales song
Push it away, feeling good
doesn't belong
In a way we create our Fate
Change we better or else
Checkmate

When the tears fall on your
guitar
Look up to the sky and stars
You may think that we're apart
But I'm really there in your heart

CHAPTER TWO

THE TRAVELER SERIES

The Traveler 1 - The Dark Light

Within the magical rays
of the universe
Is there a light that
can't be seen
The restless dawn's
tempestuousness
Within the darkness'
overshadowing

A blackness breaks
the still of day
'Twas a primary sail
on a settled sea
The compass gyrates
with the waves
The sailors luck is none to be

Pressure rising in the
atmosphere
Loss of control in a
septic spread
Landing on an exposed reef
A wake of disease
and carnal death

The spirit of incarnate kind
With a hidden enemy of desire
Pulls at the flesh its curtain call
Drives the stake with ruthless ire

The skies concede to
darkened ways
The sea maintains its
savage beasts
A vendetta in its corners stays
Until light and evil finally meet

Scales of the unjust coalesce
Bringing the darkness nigh
Awakened prior to
kindled spirits rise
The light within connects
to hypnotize

In the caverns of the nefarious
Is a place where there is no light
But omnipotent thunder
reigns supreme
That which wakes by day
and stays all night

Light breaks beyond
perpetual space
Immortal though
latent to the eye
The travelers Kevlar
skin repels the dark
Unveiling the truth of
the guiding light

The Traveler 2 - The Traveler Returns

The traveler returns
From beyond the light
A powerful force
When wrong meets right

A master of disguise
Both good and evil
Take the others mask
Question which is real

At the worlds edge
The gods are tasked
With unveiling plans
To get back the mask

And up above
In the atmosphere
The war unfolds
And the lightning's near

The sound of thunder
From unstable air
The universe shakes
With consternation and despair

Without knowing
Which way was up
He jabbed at the dark
Til his cutlass got stuck

Atomic clouds
And molecular form
The fibers exploded
And the mask was torn

And the traveler with
The Orphean mind
A musician and poet
From another time

Opportunity to save her
The chance he took
Grabbing her hand
Then back he looked

But with the glance
The deal ended
And 'halos' won
Love suspended

A coalescence
Of dark and light
Air and space
Day and night

Now he gazes ahead
And not behind
Traveling amongst
Space and time

Destiny thwarted
When the dome turned black
And his burden lifted
When he went back

Aurora colored
The darkened sky
Then she was there
When it got light

It changed the traveler
And his life indeed
For the mask he wore
He didn't need

The Traveler 3 - The Traveler's Light

His face is flesh
No more mask to hide
The very truth
He used to fight

He had been scarred
From head to toe
The lies the mirror   .
Often told

He believed
Not what he saw
But in his mind
It's what he thought

An unconscious feeling
Of diffidence
The mask allowing
Omnipotence

He was called light
And stood for good
And fought the darkness
No one else could

Throughout the universe
She knew who he was
But didn't expect
To be overcome with love

Still her darkness
Fought his light
A clash for centuries
A beguiled fight

Taking place
In the atmosphere
A thundering of blows
Was all one could hear

A fierce entanglement
To save their values' core
Became a seductive dance
Neither could ignore

Now each confused
For their lifelong quest
To rid the world
Of the other's mess

Tempted by lust
Differences set aside
But would she be the end
Of his light

They came together
The light and dark
Which began to unveil
A million stars

The darkness brought
Untold happiness
Though his bright light
Would kill Eurydice

The Traveler 4 - Power Or Love

Now without
His mask and sword
No reluctance
At this open door

He walked in
Without yield
Somewhat naked
With no mask or shield

When dark and light
Secure a bond
Will enlightenment
Still be as strong

Though gray skies
Are now prevailing
Is this the beginning
Of the travelers failing

As the light and darkness
Intertwined
The stars came out
At night and shined

They had been hidden
Behind a dark cloth
For centuries as
The forces fought

Like the traveler
The stars didn't know
Just how much
Of themselves to show

Did they bring darkness
To the light
Or did light bring darkness
To the sky

The traveler took
A breath and paused
He knew the destruction
His light could cause

A utopic encounter
Now with regret
He knew all this
Could cause her death

It had been known
From the very first hour
The good light would have
All of the power

And should he unite
With the dark side
It would be her death
And it would change his life

Now the traveler
Would have to choose
Power or love
Which one to lose

The Traveler 5 - The Beginning or the End

The traveler had to choose
And that was his sorrow
What to do now
For all tomorrows

Power or love
Til eternity
He had to decide
Which would it be

Would he ask advice
When looking in the mirror
Or was that something
That he still feared

He put the decision on hold
Til he could think rationally
He still had to light
All of the galaxy

He stepped away for a while
From the lust of Eurydice
But before he left
He gave her a kiss

And when he did
Stars began to shimmer and
shine
Why couldn't the rules be
different
Since the beginning of time

He sat on a star
Overlooking the view
As the sky was now gray
Not with dark or light hues

He wondered about
The future of it all
He felt once again
That he had hit a wall

Another obstacle
He knew very well
From the time of the mask
His own personal hell

What should he do
Where would he go
He was in love with Eurydice
That he did know

But by being with her
She would certainly die
But was this law of nature
All a lie

For this answer
He'd have to travel far away
But was he willing
To tempt fate

The Traveler 6 - The Visit to Nebula

The traveler arrived at the alpha of nebula
And proceeded through the relativity gate
He was searching for insight and answers
What all the others eventually called fate

Nebula was an endless celestial body
A little known clandestine place
The beginning of all where all began
A broader definition of time and space

Here, both time and space are infinite
Where divinity reigns supreme
Reality and deception never meet
And they're more than what they seem

Deception was dark and bad
Though she was seductively cunning
Outwardly a tumultuous affect
While inside she was always running

Anger besieged her many layers
Brought about by eons of dissent
Conflicted ways and a dark past
She had an inner desire to lament

Through the ultimate light and power
Under a great spectrum he came to be
A shield and mask he later donned
He became known as Reality

A great guardian and defender
Of all that was good and right
A birthright bestowed upon him
An historical righteous light

The traveler called upon the elders nigh
Each who were older than time
All a part of a forgotten universe
That only he was able to find

Orpheus chose to be direct
And asked about his light and power
He was reminded of a long ago pledge
Made during time's darkest hour

"Darkness had swept through
to eternity
But was stopped short with a
sacrifice
Light would share the skies with
darkness
But if ever they fused she'd
certainly die"

Where there is darkness
There still may be a spark
A little life within
Trying to climb out of the dark

That was the creed and he
now knew
The story he was told was
not a lie
But he had to know just one
more thing
Was that absolute or just a guide

"Absolute cannot be tempted
But if you do as you please
Your selfishness could alter fate
And the world after you could
cease"

So he thanked them for their time
As he had more insight now
He also knew what he had to do
He just didn't quite know how

He traveled back from way
beyond
Through the comets and
shooting stars
Questioning what the future will
bring
And if he already went too far

Traveling through the many
galaxies
A blending of dark and light
Would he return to Eurydice
And would she lose her life

The Traveler 7 - The Decision

The trip was long and arduous
More in his mind than anything
He didn't know what choice
to make
Or what his choice would bring

He learned a lot about himself
And how his powers came to
light
But if he chose to be with
darkness
He knew he'd have to fight

This seemed to be the
longest trip
The traveler ever made
Questioning his path of destiny
His light began to fade

Though his light it flickered
He felt more confident
But he knew with loving Eurydice
There'd be a consequence

If he chose to love and court her
She would surely die
And not only would she lose
her life
He'd have to relinquish all his
light

He decided he'd have to let
her go
Then it crossed his mind
What if he simply gave up his
light
Then could he love her one
more time

But if his light went out
Would others suffer certain death
Would he live forever filled
With guilt and much regret

There was no simple answer
Now that he found love
And his service to the others
That's what he was made of

He wanted to feel the passion
And be with Eurydice
He wanted the light and power
Which would he give up

He made his final decision
There would be no compromise
His light would live on for the
people
And he'd live a lonely life

He went to talk to Eurydice
But instead he found papyrus
scroll
"I cannot take the light from you
And you need to resume your
role"

Now the choice whether to
find her
And sweep her off her feet
Or back to being responsible
And just let her be

The Traveler
8 - Eurydice

Oh so long ago
Darkness had followed the light
She had always known
They would always fight

They were opposites
In every single way
She represented nighttime
And he represented day

He was light and good
She was dark and bad
Fighting for their own purpose
Was the basis of what they had

The fighting and differences
Went on since the beginning
All that mattered to them
Was the old concept of winning

But there was so much more
For their own that they protected
They lost a lot of themselves
Most of all perspective

She felt the need to win
And overtake his light
Take away his power
Fill the galaxy with fright

She was trained for eons
Not to compromise
Herself or the darkness
And always remain wise

She sought to bring out his worst
And pushed his buttons everyday
Patiently awaiting her win
Then her darkness would
surely stay

But something began to change
During one of their encounters
She suddenly found him
attractive
And no longer wanted to take
his power

So all the fighting gave way
To a lustful dance
Right then they decided
To give each other a chance

It helped that each ones
perspective
Had changed through the times
Neither had wanted to harm
the other
Instead they balanced out the
light

Eurydice was ready to give up
her life
For his passionate ways
But she wouldn't let him lose
his light
So she decided to stay away

The Traveler
9 - The End or
the Beginning

The travelers light quit shining
The skies grew a stormy gray
He had to let go of the
darkness
It was the only way

Before the storm there was a
calmness
And the sea had reflected his
light
Now the storm was fierce and
unending
With tumultuous seas far
and wide

His heart was broke and he
missed her
That's why his light no longer
shone
Though many millennia had
passed
He just didn't want to be alone

New stars were born and fell
As he simply plugged along
Day after day gray skies
reminded him
Maybe his decision had been
wrong

The days and nights they
blended
Others suffered from his gray
mood
No longer did any light shine
bright
Except for the stars and moon

The moon and stars they shined
Through the gray veil of life
But could he regain his power
And again give forth his light

Never before did he have power
When without the light
He always knew the two of
them
Were required for his might

He no longer had the strength
to shine
But could he muster enough
power
The universe it heard his plea
And began a meteor shower

Our traveler broke a smile
The first in many years
Now he had the power back
And he saw a future near

He continued to gain strength
As the years went on
He had his power back
But his light was still gone

He realized that his power
Had little to do with the light
And his sense of responsibility
Was no one's birthright

He knew he enjoyed doing for
others
But would take a step back
So he could see things
differently
Whenever he felt overtaxed

He went on about his business
And light gave way to gray
There was no sign of darkness
For forever and a day

Our traveler decided to take a
break
And shot right to the stars
This became his place to go
When he needed a new start

This time it was different
He got the feeling he wasn't
alone
Maybe this is just the feeling
You get when you have grown

He wasn't responsible for the
world
Though no light he still had
power
He had learned many things
In his proverbial last hour

Still he felt a presence
One he had felt before
It gave off a good energy
This time he knew for sure

While sitting on his favorite star
Looking out across the miles
Suddenly they're eyes met
He teared up when he saw her
smile

The stars now shined brighter
than ever
And the gray skies went away
Things were back to normal
There was night and there
was day

Though there is no moral
The story reminds us still
Love's a possibility
There's always a way when
there's a will

The Traveler 10
- A Look Back

Though now there was night
and day
Not everything was bliss
For they both knew their love
Could come at one huge risk

It had been drilled into both
of them
Since they were very young
They must serve out their
purpose
And never fall in love

For if they found a purpose
Different from what their
mission sought
Others would suffer the
consequences
And light or darkness would
be lost

Was each of their lives a mission
Without a purpose in the plan
For they felt if there was no
reason
Then all of this be damned

But in their youth they strived
To become strong and gain
their power
Not realizing in many millennia
They'd have to fight each other

He had to be the best
Strong but fair in all his ways
He didn't know when the
darkness
Would overshadow days

She learned the tools of
deception
And she also learned to fight
Cuz the time would eventually
come
When she needed to end his light

There was no fun or playtime
For the light or for the dark
They were simply being
groomed
To only play their part

But somewhere inside of each
Was a hint of a mood astray
A wish and a desire
Perhaps in future days

He had felt so lonely
While being taught his mission
But being alone was paramount
And for that he was conditioned

She too wanted the
companionship
Of another immortal soul
But her elders knew the
detriment
And the future was the goal

So their powers slowly
developed
Until they could get it right
She became pitch darkness
And he became the light

The Traveler 11 - Her Young Darkness

Though he believed there was
some light
Her soul was dark indeed
If he could just get her to relent
Then her darkness could be
freed

From an early start
She followed her own ways
She'd cause gray skies to darken
There was nothing anyone
could say

By the time that she was seven
She was done learning her new
skills
And over and over the elders
reiterated
Vanishing the light was her
purpose still

She took this task to heart
In fact the hellacious winds
blew wild
And though she was only nine
She was hardly considered a
child

She spent the early years
Near the edge of a black hole
Waiting for the light to show
Till darkness could take its toll

Her wrath was quite fierce
And her starkness was a
gray hue
The canvases' light grew dim
As her hatred for the Traveler
grew

But when they both first met
To settle an age-old score
They both knew in an instant
They wanted something more

Something more for each other
Instead of ending the others life
Could he tolerate her darkness
And her his sovereign light

Was it love at first sight
Or was it during their
pugnacious dance
Could they alter their destiny
Or would they have a fighting
chance

Training or not their feelings
crept
Into their conscious minds
Would they keep their feelings
out of it
Or would their feelings make
them blind

Blind about time and space
Blind about their life-long roles
Would they continue their
innate fight
Or would they give in to their
caring souls

He'd let loose of his lightening
And she let out her thunderous
boom
Then they'd fight nearly
every day
And it seemed like one of them
was doomed

The Traveler
12 - The Scar

Time nearly stood still
From the first time
that they met
Flying through the atmosphere
They tried to fight
until the death

The traveler's power and might
Were incomplete
without his sword
And he had the ability
to rationalize
Using just his words

He had a way to compromise
But she was strong
in her own way
With the ability to
burn someone
Just by what she'd say

She slung belittling words
That caught him well off guard
And in the confusion
touched his face
And left him forever scarred

Quickly he turned and left
His brightness surely dimmed
Upset he didn't defend himself
And that he let her get to him

He returned to his
place of solace
And took a look into the mirror
What he saw made
him nauseous
And filled him with utter terror

He knew he couldn't
face the truth
As he had let himself down
He felt like such a forgery
Til a mask that he would don

From then on he'd wear it
His face he'd want to hide
The mask it hid his scars
And the tears within his eyes

But the thing about his face
Through all his fear and dread
Not a single flaw was showing
It was all just in his head

The Traveler 13 - His Physical Truth

The beauty of the universe
And the appearance of space
Captivated the viewers eyes
As did his gently rugged face

The Traveler's perception went
beyond
What was seen by the eye
Except when it came to him
And the scar he couldn't deny

He saw it in the mirror
He felt it with his hand
He knew it in his heart
His insecurities began

For him it was more than
physical
She had cut him to the quick
Her words had cut right
through him
And made him very sick

"All you are is light
My darkness will always reign
You can't protect anyone
Cuz I'll bring you down again"

"You call yourself a man
But you're no more than a fake
Full of righteous indignation
Give up now for your people's
sake"

"When you look into the mirror
You'll know who's more
supreme
Give up your light and sword
Your power's nothing but a
dream"

She laughed as he went away
Her darkness now more than
pitch
He knew he had to return
And his tactics he'd have to
switch

The mask was now a part
of him
As acrimony didn't suit him well
He worked on himself for many
moons
And on his face he would not
dwell

He wasn't a vain immortal man
And if the truth be told
It wasn't a physical scar that
threw him
It was the darkness of her soul

The Traveler 14 - The Power of Light

The power of his
sword and shield
Were helped by the
mask he wore
And the nature of the
light within him
Made him powerful all the more

This little fact not known
To our Traveler's conscious mind
On the surface he was a warrior
Down deep his soul was kind

Though there was no
reason to wear it
The mask made him
more secure
Cuz he didn't believe
in his power within
Though the light was
his strength for sure

He never wanted to be a warrior
Though he did like
being the light
He didn't see darkness
as the enemy
And he had a fear of
ending her night

That wasn't the only fear he had
Or the only pain that
he endured
For many years he wrestled with
Who he saw when
looking in the mirror

But that was not his
current issue
He felt conflicted in his ways
If he filled the destiny
of his people
It would be the end of
the darkness's days

With this he really struggled
But the light had to
continue to shine
So when he went into battle
He was less than kind

Through the many years
They fought numerous times
They both eventually realized
Without the other they
were lost in time

Then the inevitable clash
With the sea and darkened skies
The power of light
beyond the dark
Became known as the dark light

The Traveler 15 - The Coming Together

Now it seemed they had it all
But he was still without his light
They both had grown infinitely
And had gained so much insight

Originally their future
was all mapped out
Way before their birth
Each was to take the
other down
Then one would reign the earth

He would stand for
good and hope
And be the forever light
She would ensure the
darkened ways
And stand for what's not right

But things started to
change early on
When something primal
was struck within
It was then they started to see
Perhaps there could
be a different end

Yes they fought but
more than that
They got to know each
other's strengths
And maybe more important still
Was how to help the
other weakness

Though he was day
and she was night
And opposites they were
Opponents of the dark and light
One complements the other

No longer was there
a choice to make
Their love would certainly win
They would seek the
elders' blessings
Then their lives together
would begin

The Traveler 16 - Permission

Together they went to Nebula
And asked his elders permission
Which was granted pretty quickly
Though not originally their vision

Orpheus would retain his light
A gift for his good ways
And the elders welcomed Eurydice
The start of brighter days

Onto the planetary darkened side
They had hoped to take a stand
by pledging their reciprocal commitment
Instead she was forever banned

Eurydice was deeply saddened
Though she was not disheartened
Because she was most in love
And their life together just started

Constellations shone brightly
And the stars danced till dawn
It seemed like all the rivalry
Was finally all gone

An enlightened celebration
And some even came to support the dark
This was a day for the future books
And their personal journey would start

The Traveler 17 - Forever Light

As the universe it watched
And the comets did their thing
The stars twinkled brightly
Harmony would sing

They had finally made it
Despite all the odds
They were truly happy
And so were all the gods

Their love it was pronounced
Then it was set in motion
For all the universe
And the life within the ocean

There was a light and a quake
But there was no fear
Because everything the world needed
Was finally right here

With the final blessing
And the ceremony done
He was granted the ultimate
He became the sun

She was no longer darkness
No more a sense of doom
She became the light in the dark
She became the moon

Forever they'd be together
A light for eternity
Perhaps from the beginning
They were meant to be

The Traveler
18 - The Twin

They lived through the era
A new birth you could say
A time of coalescence
Each beautiful new day

The universe was still
And the kestrel did hark
A light was now showing
In the midst of the dark

But the dilated pupil
Of the eagle hawk's sharp eye
Signaled that something
Must certainly be awry

A signal of a change
And the skies began to turn
Even as the sun rose
The horizon appeared to burn

The hues colored the vastness
And the seas were stormy too
The volcanoes lost their
dormancy
And darkness seemed to loom

The shaking of the land
Sent shivers down the spine
From the darkened past
And not from modern times

There was heaviness in the air
But what could bring such weight
Certainly it couldn't be the
brother
Who was filled with fervid hate

He died as a young man
But perhaps his spirit rose
The Traveler looked identical
when the two would juxtapose

You see they were twins
And the two of them were close
It had been an accident
As everybody knows

It occurred while searching
Along the oceans sand
It was as though someone
Just grabbed him with their
hand

The Traveler 19 - Brother Admyion

The brothers had been
searching
For rocks along the shore
They had found a bucketful
But the brother wanted more

The rocks were from a place
And a time of long ago
They lit up the darkness
And gave meteors their glow

They had been inundated
With a shower earlier that year
But when the Traveler said
enough
The brother couldn't hear

The Traveler was the oldest
His brother was born deaf
They had been alone
Since their parents left

His name was Admyion
And it meant silent sound
He had an inner strength
That made his skills profound

But that day along the shoreline
When everything grew dark
He's was plucked up by the air
And taken to afar

So much time had passed
That the Traveler thought he
died
And for many centuries
Orpheus let out his cries

He couldn't live without him
So he stuffed the nightmare
down
The memory of his brother
Could no longer be found

While he was gone
Admyion believed his fear
That his brother was the one
Who made him disappear

He honed his essential skills
After he had been taken away
He trained with the dark
Waiting for this day

The Traveler 20 - Brothers No More

Although the shaking stopped
The volcanoes puffed their smoke
It was as if
The earth finally awoke

But it wasn't before
The sky turned to black
Orpheus had seen this before
He knew the darkness was back

He couldn't believe that
Admyion
Would turn to the dark side
Down deep he knew
That something wasn't right

And For her safety
He sent Eurydice in flight
She would go to Nebula
In case there was a fight

The traveler knew his light
strength
Would his brother run with fear
He had known his only
weakness
Though it seemed Admyion
could hear

As the traveler approached
But before he drew his sword
Admyion just looked at him
And seemed to mouth some
words

Admyion had never spoke
So it caught Orpheus off guard
Had something changed
When he was taken to the stars

But what was it exactly
That Admyion was trying to say
Should Orpheus get closer
Or should he play it safe

He decided to trust his kin
And as he moved up closer
Admyion said the words
"I am not your brother"

With that Admyion jumped
On Orpheus' backside
He then took out a dagger
And jabbed it in his side

The Traveler
21 - Fear

Due to the horrible pain
Orpheus stumbled back
But more than the pain
He was quite aghast

Who would ever think
Twins as close as they
Would ever be fighting
To the death this way

Orpheus grabbed the dagger
And to Admyion he said
My brother what turned you
against me
And why do you want me dead

In a gruff and raspy voice
Admyion did say
I stopped being your brother
When I was taken from here
that day

Now Orpheus bleeding badly
Was quite confused indeed
You've been turned by the
darkness
They've filled you with hate
for me

We have always been close
You are my younger twin
We will always be brothers
Through thick and thin

You are not to blame
Your anger speaks louder than
words
They filled your head with hate
Don't believe what you heard

You were born deaf
Not a sound could you hear
They used that against you
And exposed your every fear

Now your hate and rage
Make you someone that
you're not
We'll have it removed
That which the darkness
brought

Admyion wasn't interested
In what Orpheus just said
For I can hear now
The darkness is my friend

As Orpheus plead his case
The volcano began to spew
The ocean's tide it turned
And the skies grew darker too

Since you can now hear me
Please listen to what I say
I've been your only friend
Since our parents went away

You always stood your ground
Whether I was there or not
You simply used your charm
You never even fought

When others picked on you
Because you didn't speak
And they called you names
You were never weak

You fought through the fear
Because you always knew
It's not what you're called
It's what you answer to

The Traveler 22 - Together They Stand

Admyion believed
Orpheus' words
He fought the dark inside
Believing what he heard

He fell to his knees
As Orpheus fell to the ground
They knew it would be
okay now
For the key they had found

They knew from childhood
That when one was afraid
To call upon the light
Tomorrow's another day

With that the darkness
Began the mighty wrath
And brought a sense of
darkness
The land never had

Though Orpheus was hurt
Together they took a stand
United they'd win this fight
Admyion took his hand

The Traveler's light shone
Through darkness' evil ways
Like stars through a canvas
The dawn of a new day

But the evil was strong
And Orpheus was weak
But he gave it his all
So they could live free

And using his newly found
voice
To the darkness Admyion said
You gave me a voice for evil
But I'll use it for good instead

Evil wasn't happy
The skies grew darker still
The land began to shake
Then everything stood still

There certainly would be a
battle
Unlike one had ever seen
Sometimes it takes a challenge
To understand what's serene

The Traveler 23 - A Challenge to Change

Admyion knew all too well
How challenges can be rough
After all he lived most of his life
Totally mute and deaf

Sometimes going through
rough times
Reminds us we're still strong
Even though we might feel
Like giving up when things go
wrong

As the battle raged on
The brothers stood as one
And after several moons
They just wanted it to be done

Orpheus' light still shined
As Admyion began to orate
He tried to convince the
darkness
That violence was not the way

But that's all the darkness knew
The evil and wicked ways
And he didn't know how to let
Goodness change those ways

Orpheus now barely
hanging on
Cried out one last plea
"Do what is right for all
And let the violent battle cease"

"There's no place in this world
For any kind of fight
Give up your evil forever
And begin to follow what's
right"

The darkness thought about it
And vacillated between good
and evil
He thought about how life did
change
And thought about all the
people

Darkness was actually tired
From keeping up a life so mean
But that's all he had known
Since the very beginning

Changing for the better
It's never too late to begin
Leaving evil behind
You win when you make the
decision

Since darkness turned to good
And changed his wicked ways
The whole entire expansive
universe
Was made better that very day

The Traveler 24 - The Next Chapter

The concession of the darkness
To now do good and right
Revealed another great one
Like that of Orpheus' light

The darkness became a fixture
And the light became a source
For good instead of evil
A part of the right force

Now Orpheus grew stronger
With every passing day
It also helped that Eurydice
Was home to stay

Admyion thanked his brother
Then left for his new home
He wanted to give Eurydice and
Orpheus
Time to be alone

They enjoyed their time
together
For their health they felt blessed
Eurydice took care of Orpheus
As he convalesced

It didn't take long for him to
get well
And the light shined bright again
He felt stronger than ever
Especially from where he
had been

This was a special time
Full of good instead of bad
For Orpheus and Eurydice
Were about to be mom
and dad

Eurydice woke one morning
And saw her face aglow
That is about the time
That she came to know

Orpheus she said
I've something to make you glad
In several more months
You're going to be a dad

He was quite over the moon
And it only seemed a little while
Till Eurydice gave birth
To a beautiful child

CHAPTER THREE

A Clouded Mind

In the days of old
We could all dance
And celebrate milestones
Then with a glance

I noticed your eyes
so empty and lost
In the time of a deep breath
You had already crossed

Into another place
where I could not reach you
A different destination
Is where you went to

The rain comes pouring down
Like the tears that I cry
Oh the memory of
what used to be
And of what life was like

Yesterday's gone and
tomorrow's a dream
Now there's clouds in your mind
Leaving us all to wonder
Is there any part of
you left behind

You slipped away to a land
A place that's far away
Where I don't live or exist
And things are what you make

I only hope that you feel safe
And are surrounded by
thoughts that care
Although they're only
in your mind
No one else can help you there

Be safe my love til
again we know
Who each other are
Then we'll talk until eternity
And hold each other
in our arms

A Four Letter Word

It's all about adversity
Misfortune claiming you
For some it's a four letter word
A challenge to rise to

The word may be luck
That somehow you're still alive
The word may be hope
Helping you to survive

Perhaps the word fate
Is what comes to mind
Undoubtedly the word lost
Can lead to the word find

A Quiet Place

A quiet place to go
Where I can take a stroll
Where everything is real
And anything can go

I close my eyes and see
All the beauty in my mind
I can make it what I want
A paradise I find

A real relaxing place
No one to bother me
Pleasant scenery
And being totally free

It only ends when I say
And blue skies appear above
When I open my eyes
And all I feel is love

A Stranger's Shoes

I don't have a place to call home
And I don't have a roof over my
head
I don't know when I'll get to
shower
Or the next time I'll even be fed

You see I'm what they call
homeless
I don't have a place to live
I have nothing but this cart full
of stuff
And I rely on people that give

I can't ever get comfortable
And I cannot crawl into a
warm bed
When I go to bed the insects
and rats
Crawl in with me instead

Now I'm sick and not well
To top it off there's a winter
storm
I try to brave the elements
But sometimes I wish I hadn't
been born

Perhaps I'll hear a hello today
I can barely look when a
stranger walks by
Maybe they'll give me a dollar
or two
I hope they just don't roll
their eyes

It's not like this is what I
asked for
Drugs and alcohol are not my
thing
I'm not lazy and I'm not no good
But I know that's what some
people think

To not have food and be
hungry
To not have a drink but to thirst
To trade one day with another
I'd trade you my best for your
worst

I have this tarp to keep my
things dry
I don't think of what I have not
I have some cardboard I use
as a mat
And I'm grateful for what I've got

You see I learned long ago
There's more to life than things
To get a warm feeling in my
heart
That is what your kindness brings

Though it's difficult most of
the time
I feel things no one else can
But I wouldn't walk in another's
shoes
However ironically every day I am

A Whisper of Time

To have you back for a day
With a clear mind
With words coming easy
Not ones that you have to find

To have you back for an hour
The conversation we would have
Of yesterday, today, or tomorrow
I wouldn't be aggravated or sad

To have you back for a minute
The looks we would share
We'd focus on the now
And just enjoying being near

To have you back for right now
I'd look into your eyes
And see what we've still got
Not my usual cries

To just hold your hand
Or to dance a dance
Just a second or two
If we only had the chance

To be with the person
I once had known
For just a whisper of time
You wouldn't be alone

We once had it all
In a way we still do
I wish the you inside
Could forever break through

Adversity

It's a battle of one
You and adversity
But as long as you hold steadfast
You'll never be free

When the dove is left alone
And has cried all its tears
It takes to flight once again
And faces all it's fear

We could learn a lot
From this lonesome bird
As it flies again
Though still lonely and scared

Alone I Stand

I stand on the mountain high
I stand with my feet in the sand
I stand for what's right and good
I find alone I stand

Alone I stand with you
Alone I stand as one
Alone I stand with me
I just want to run

I just want to run
Until I reach the end
Then I stand alone
And do it all again

I stand in the mud
I stand in the rain
I stand on a rock
I stand alone in pain

Alone Together

We may be alone together
But we're worlds apart
I am at the finish line
And you are at the start

We all have a story to tell
And they're all different
Some long some short some good or bad
But all of them are meant

Meant to be your story
Though It may be a cross you bear
Perhaps it's about adversity
Or of how you're always scared

Perhaps you won the lotto
And money fixed it all
But even if a pauper
You can still stand tall

You don't have to be alone
Though the feeling deep inside
You fight the battle of one
It's the battle you choose to fight

You may just feel less challenged
If you let it go
But if you don't surrender
Then you'll never know

Alone

I've been alone in the ocean
With sharks all around
And bleeding tears
No hope to be found

I've been alone in the forest
Looking up seeing trees
Not even the sky
Looked down on me

I've been alone in a dream
Unable to wake
But I prayed before bedtime
God my soul please take

I've been alone in life
Day after day
No visible sores
But in horrific pain

I've been alone in my mind
For so many years
There's no escaping
It's my book of fears

I've been alone in a crowd
In a room full of friends
Waiting for the funeral
To finally end

I'm alone all the time
At least in my mind
It's not the loneliness
I'm trying to fight

You see it's the no hope
On down the line
It tells me to give up
All of the time

It says nothing will change
And that it will only worsen
It seems like a disease
Going from person to person

Feeling like there's no hope
Is like not having a name
And when you're alone with
no hope
It's the end of the game

Ambivalent Love

A pattern of ambivalent love
Fault merely a word to make one think
Innocence when stuck and chained
Evil water from which he'd drink

A youth so quiet for it was known
Telling would ruin the surprise
Never a whisper to be told
Though swallowing hard and crying eyes

Slapped with the hand of a madman
Coddled by the same hand that holds
Left feeling ambivalent for his love
Nothing changed as he'd grow old

She'd not speak of the brewing storm
That often caught her face
Her hair tousled from the dance
On dark nights and wind whipped days

She had a friend and they stayed strong
But there were others too
All the tiptoeing around the storm
Paralyzed none could make a move

It came down to being free
From the mental chains inflicted
It meant without help from all
Their sanity was slowly evicted

She said the truth that she was told not to
And with that she was saved
Goodbye to the madman that she loved
And wandered off with but a wave

As I Say Goodbye

Your will is strong
But your voice is weak
I take care of you
But you're thinking of me

You're worried that
I'll be left alone
And what will I do
When you're gone

I reassure you
That I'll do fine
The hurt will heal
All in good time

I thank you
For all you've done
For who you are
For who I've become

I'll always love you
No matter where you are
And I'll keep a part of you
Right here in my heart

And as I say goodbye
And you take your last breath
You won't be leaving me
In your death

Cuz when you're an angel
Learning to fly
You'll watch over me
Till the end of time

As You Age

It's hard to watch
As you grow older
Your health declines
And your hands grow colder

You're not as nimble
And you start to slip
You're a little slower
And you begin to forget

If your vision gets bad
And you can no longer hear
And your gait is unsteady
Just know I'll be there

I know it's hard to accept
That you're not quite as strong
When you have felt able
Through the years all along

Though it may be harder to think
I hope your mind is at ease
Especially if one day
You don't remember me

Comfort in your heart
And peace of mind
Is what I wish for you
Cuz you've given me mine

Bobby's Kite

When I was young
I flew a kite
And when I'd run
It'd go real high

It was like
An innocence
That later in life
Made perfect sense

I didn't know
When I held that string
It was really a rope
To your guillotine

I let go
Cuz I couldn't hold on
You were not weak
And I was not strong

I've always felt the guilt
My selfishness caused
And ever since then
I've felt totally lost

Your map of life
Led off the page
And you went off-roading
To a different place

To a different stage
A place that's safe
A stage of confusion
Is where I stayed

And I'd often wonder
If you knew
Or know now
What I think of you

A brave soul
Up in the sky
Not weak like me
When I fly my kite

Bully

As a bully
You prey on the weak
You have a problem
And it goes pretty deep

Who would gang up
On innocent folks
Make up lies about them
And make them the butt of your jokes

You call them names
Oh my you're so tough
You ditch them at school
And treat them so rough

You're just a big bully
But really you are insecure
You make fun of others
And you really don't care

The biggest jerk around
That is what defines you
You just think you're real cool
Deep down you know it's not true

Fighting others smaller than you
You think you're so strong
But you're just a coward
And your behavior is wrong

I believe
That you'll get yours one day
Maybe not on this earth
But when God has his say

Buzzards

Inside the belly of the whale
Within the blue and white walls
Waiting for the next big breath
Thinking I've said it all

Outside the buzzards wait atop a tree
And watch the people throw their stones
The big black birds just biding their time
Till they can pick clean my bones

The stones are made of yesterday's mess
And always a new one follows
Grabbing in and pulling out my heart
While in their lack of apathy they wallow

Perhaps they don't know their power
Or how the rocks' sharp edges maim
But maybe if they did know
They'd just do it all again

The family of buzzards waiting for the call
When whilst my body is no longer leased
They've taken all but what's left
Now they enjoy the anticipated feast

Remnants left for rats and ants
Of what was once so wise
Seeing beyond its own self
Everything lives and everything dies

Before its clock strikes most of the time
Prior to its state of readiness
Unending appetite and a hand is out
They brought it to its untimely death

Cancer

How dare you
Try to take my life
You scare me too
But I'll survive

You also bring
A false pre-conception
You hope I'll falter
At your mere mention

Shocked at first
But I know me well
I'll fight to your death
You can go to hell

Never giving up
That's the answer
When you're fighting
A type of cancer

Chained 1- Personal Chains

I'm chained to my past
No matter where I go
I walk around in circles
I've never been able to grow

Always acting as though
I need to be someone else
Never being satisfied
Just being myself

If I chew off my foot
Will I really be free
But if I leave the chain on
I can't ever be

Such a dilemma
Like life as a whole
Life is like living
In a rabbit hole

You stray too far
Fate pulls you back
Is it because we're actually
Riding through life on a track

Was it all arranged
Before we were born
Is being an individual
No more than folklore

Something to think about
Maybe these chains aren't locked
Perhaps I have the key
To this sinister plot

Chained 2-
The Track

We're all on a track
And our lives are controlled
From when we're quite young
Till the time that we're old

Our life's pre-determined
And all arranged
I know this sounds crazy
And pretty strange

Are we the greyhound
Running on a track
Or are we the rabbit
That never looks back

Are we all horses
On a carousel ride
Is this life about
Biding our time

Whatever the case
Whichever the view
There's nothing at all
That we can do

Or is there something
We can do to change things
And be in charge
Of what our life brings

Who knows the truth
When nothing seems right
Maybe we're being led around
Throughout this life

Do we have choice
It would seem so
But is the outcome controlled
Like a Hollywood show

Is this the stopover
Between death and eternity
Some would even call this
Purgatory

Chained 3- Just the Facts

Is 'life' but a stop
On the road to forever
Or is this all we get
A fruitless endeavor

Is there a master or group
That controls our views
Our thoughts and actions
Our every move

Is it all "fake news"
As some have said
Will it all end
At the time of our death

Is there a man behind a curtain
Or someone pulling the strings
Is there an option
To what life will bring

Do we have choices
Do we have a say
Are these all questions
That will be answered one day

Do we get the message
Are we on the right track
Is life interpretation
Rather than facts

I think in the end
It's what you want it to be
It's about how you live
And what you believe

Color in Times of Darkness

It was in my darkest moment
That I fully realized
I felt feelings more Intensely
From laughing to teary eyed

The walls came crumbling down
It's the moment next to death
When I feel the most extreme
And like there's nothing left

I can't explain the contradiction
It's like 20/20 vision zoomed in
So very clear and larger
than life
Simply waiting for the end to
begin

I force myself to continue
To feel the unbridled agony
Perhaps it belonged to another
But it also just feels like me

I take on others' traumas
And the bad times in their life
Times of fear and anxiety
And certainly times of strife

Feeling empathy for others
Or my own experiencing of it
It's color in times of darkness
A most unusual gift

A gift or a curse
It feels more dark than good
More sensitive to feelings
Perhaps more than it should

Color comes thru at the bleak
times
An intensity when there should
be none
Does that keep one going back
for more
Or is it just another step on
the rung

In mystery and self control
The ladder of life abounds
The abilities of the body
and mind
Is inner strength lost or found

The color of darkness
Rich in feelings and hues
Brings about a chance to see
And perhaps a change in you

Death

You show up to my door
Wanting to talk
I tell you I'm not ready
You say let's take a walk

We wander to the cliffs
You show me a new home
It's just to the south
Up from the ocean

Outside the fresh air
We venture to the sand
You convince me
That I should take your hand

So we make our plans
And pick out a date
Maybe this time you'll show up
And maybe I won't be late

Now it's on the eve
And it's dark outside
Gown is hanging in the closet
I'm thinking that it's right

I tried not to get roped in
When you came
knocking at my door
It all left me with a headache
That's what the pills are for

Now you're cold as ice
At the party I go stag
And the van backs up
I'm laid out like a rag

We really tied one on
A knot that's strong and all
One that will not break
When I start to fall

Now in a new home
The nightmare it begins
When you open the door
To someone you think's a friend

Dream a Little Dream

As I lay my head
And I try to rest
Just a little peace
That is my request

Sometimes I go to sleep
Which takes me far away
To a place I don't know
A place where I'm afraid

I fall into a void
A black hole in mind space
From which there's no escape
A matrix of time and place

A state of the unconscious
A corner within the depths
Where visions, thoughts, and
words
Touch the edge of death

Locus of control is lost
Direction rather random
Falling deeper towards the
confines
With no ability to abandon

Falling farther into
fragmentation
No sense to what it means
Come to before hitting the wall
Welcome to your dreams

It gives the being rest
Mind, body, and soul
Realization of going somewhere
For which there's no control

A room for rejuvenation
Oil for a rusty mind
A locale we visit often
But while awake we cannot find

When you yell and there's no
sound
There's a fear that travels inside
And a sense of doom
Am I about to die

A threat to your life
Perhaps teeth falling out
A fall into the vastness
Or flying pleasantly about

What if we don't come back
From this mind box that we're in
And we don't wake up
Is this now where we begin

There's no avoiding that place
Where fears and pleasantries
collide
That dimension that makes for
our sanity
Or allows insanity to hide

Fear

Fear
You paralyze
You keep me from moving
You tell me lies

You tell me that I'll get hurt
Or that it's all my fault
And it's better to leave it closed
That memory vault

You don't want me to venture
Out on a limb
You tell me to stay
Out of the ocean

You don't want me
To have any fun
You keep telling me
Bad's gonna come

You make me fear
Taking a chance
It's as though you have me
In a trance

But no more
Cuz I want to live
And so I'll walk
Along the edge

Flying In a Chopper

Flying in a chopper
But we can't get off the ground
There's wires overhead
No freedom to be found

Hoping for an open space
To be able to soar
But kept from the autonomy
Because of a personal war

A battle that gets fought
Every single day
With triumph so elusive
The trying to twist fate

We're not meant to be free
In our mind or for real
We're stuck with what is
No more trying to feel

The little battlefields of life
Are the most difficult
We just keep on fighting them
Without the wanted result

Wanting different outcomes
But doing the same thing
That's what we do in life
And it makes us a little insane

Are our actions predetermined
And the outcome sealed
Cuz hoping for different results
Is all but real

Buzzard Family

Who knew they were vultures
They hid it skillfully
As they quietly picked among the bones
Nearly surgically

The heart it still beat
And the body was still warm
But they took turns pulling at the flesh
All done so uniform

As the rain kept falling
And the heart rate slowed in pace
They gnawed even more impatiently
As others took their place

Soon the beat it stopped
As they plucked out every hair
The carcass soon faded away
For it no longer cared

Now soaring in the sky
Miles high can see
The buzzards still pick the bones
In the dry desert heat

I Pray For Ya (To the tune of "Hallelujah")

You gave to me the gift of life
And taught me all about the Light
And how He always hears and
listens to ya
You held my hand and let
me know
You'd still be there when you let
it go
And I'll be there as I pray for ya

I pray for ya
I pray for ya
I pray for ya
I pray for ya

You'd stay up with me through
the night
When I was sick or filled with
fright
And you wouldn't leave until
you said I love ya
When I fell to the ground from
the tree
You put a bandage on my
knees
And with a kiss you'd simply say
I love ya

I pray for ya
I pray for ya
I pray for ya
I pray for ya

The Book it told of His story
And you told of His glory
And how one day He'd be right
there before ya
And now with tired eyes you see
A different kind of beauty
The kind that seems to only be
there for ya

I pray for ya
I pray for ya
I pray for ya
I pray for ya

And though you're in a
weakened state
You believe and still have faith
That now I can do it all for ya
I take your hand in my hand
We walk although you cannot
stand
You're stronger now as I help
and lead ya

I pray for ya
I pray for ya
I pray for ya
I pray for ya

I Pray to Ya (To the tune of "Hallelujah")

Was there a time when things
were fair
And love and truth were not
so rare
And hope was there by
reaching out to ya
As a child when things were fun
And as a grown up life begun
And whispers meant that I was
praying to ya

I pray to ya
I pray to ya
I pray to ya
I pray to ya

I look up above and cry a tear
And most of what I feel is fear
I don't know how to get
closer to ya
I read the Book and know the
rules
But I'm sad cuz the world is cruel
And I don't know how to help
out but do ya

I pray to ya
I pray to ya
I pray to ya
I pray to ya

This sadness cuts right to my core
And I don't know what you're
waiting for
You don't want me hurting
more do ya
I hope you hear my plea this time
And happiness you make it mine
But now I just want to be near ya

I pray to ya
I pray to ya
I pray to ya
I pray to ya

I'm at a place it's dark in here
And the world for me I just
can't bear
Oh Lord I really really do
need ya
I'm in so much pain but I
really try
I won't give up but I cannot fight
I'm afraid but I keep on
praying to ya

I pray to ya
I pray to ya
I pray to ya
I pray to ya

Giving Up

The oceans tide will bring
The sand under your feet
But in a violent storm
It'll take it back to sea

The lightning brings the
thunder
Or the thunder brings the light
Does the fight bring the
challenge
Or does the challenge bring the
fight

The lion with no voice
Is no longer king
A bird without a song
Can no longer sing

A fenced yard with no gate
A dog without a bone
A story without words
A man without a home

Lost in oneself
Not to mention lost in life
Brings a sense of hopelessness
And swallowing of pride

A tug and a pull
You give it all you've got
It's only as good as the beam
When the support is full of rot

The seed was planted long ago
But water it did lack
So it went into dormancy
Till the day it would come back

It grew rather quietly
And festered inside
And took all the adrenaline
Right out of the fight

Now soaring in the sky
Miles high can see
The buzzards pick the bones
In the dry desert heat

I Stand Alone

I stand alone
With you by my side
In a crowd
When things go right

I stand alone
For I've pushed all away
While still longing for
companionship
I guess I was afraid

Afraid of what I don't know
Afraid of eventually
being left alone
Afraid of feeling
something anything
I stand alone

And in the final line
Where crowds have
gathered to answer
I stand alone
Waiting for the Creator

Again I stand alone
Though the Creator I'm
standing before
I closed all the windows I could
And I locked every door

And as I get set to answer
I take a look around
They've all gone away
No one left to be found

I stand alone
Poised at the ready
But He doesn't ask
me any questions
Instead He just hugs me

Do I still stand alone
For all of my eternity
I indeed stand alone
And I want to be free

Life As a Tree

I watch the tree
In the storm
And how it bends
From its natural form

With gusts so strong
It begins to break
But within its roots
A new life it'll make

For the fallen part
It feeds the ground
Sustenance for insects
Destiny bound

Though it's broken
It doesn't end
With a little time
It will mend

It may not be
The same as before
Though different
Perhaps stronger

Like a colorful arch
That comes after a rain
When something's broken
New growth can begin

One may be fragile
Of body or mind
But like a tree can mend
All in good time

My Angel

You became an angel
The moment that you left
You glided up to Heaven
To be with the very best

You're sitting on a cloud
Watching from high above
You always meant so much to me
I was lucky to have your love

You're absolutely missed
With your own unique ways
I know I'll see you again
I just have to have faith

Nothing by Chance

Listen up to what you hear
Nothing by chance
Meant to be from world's unknown
When you meet and do the dance

To elicit thought and action
For your future days
Throwing fear and stagnation aside
The universe turns in symbiotic ways

As the flow of what's right comes together
And what could be rains down
One lives their best here and now
No longer lost but to be found

Life Stars

Another star was switched off
It had burned brightly for years
And it lighted a distant universe
Now a trail like an exposed nerve

Seen speeding thru the sky
Since the time of its birth
Once vibrant and full of life
Now it's fallen to the earth

When another star dies out
Does hope go with it
When another life runs out
Is that it

In the times of a remote before
Big dreams they did surmount
Did they mean anything
Or did they even count

The good deeds
Done for so long
Now does suddenly
This mean it was wrong

And the life
Of the star in the sky
When the switch is flipped
Does it all become a lie

When another star dies out
Does hope go with it
When another life runs out
Is that it

Is it just a black canvas
With LED's behind
Are the stars simply holes
In the canvas of the mind

And is the light that is the
moon
Just a tear within the sheet
Wipe your eyes and wait your
turn
And don't cheat

And is it just a hole
Where the sun shines
Is it a faceless clock
That tells no time

When another star dies out
Hope goes with it
When another life runs out
That's it

Turn the light off

My Walk

I can no longer hear
When others talk
I've turned a deaf ear
As I start my walk

I don't want to listen
To your reasons why
As you try to convince me
That I don't want to die

I know that down deep
In my gut way inside
Things are too painful
So I'll run and hide

Actually it's a walk
And I take it all in
Listening to the agony
And hurting again

In my right hand
I have a match
Living to die
There is no catch

You fool yourselves
Thinking there's more
But there's only pain
Behind each of the doors

In my other hand
It's ready to ignite
Just like life
It's always a fight

Always a battle
And putting out fires
Life means so little
Some see it as dire

My time is now limited
As I light the fuse
You are on your own
You get what you choose

But do we make any choice
Or is it already arranged
Do we have any control
Do we have any say

Either way
When the hurt runs so deep
You can no longer see
You can only weep

Then there are no more tears
They're all wiped dry
Hope is what you prayed for
But peace is what you find

Life's Abyss

Something's missing
It's a feeling of emptiness
A lifetime voyage
Into the great visceral abyss

There's absolutely nothing
But a vastness inside
And all the salt water in the world
For the tears that are cried

There's no filling the hole
With anything but
All of the pain
That wrenches the gut

Pain and emptiness
In a deep dark hole
Leads to a lifetime of loneliness
Like time with no soul

My War

I trained and fought
For you and me
I went to war
So we'd be free

Upon return
I wasn't treated well
Some even said
I would go to hell

"You killed the innocent
Even little kids"
It didn't seem to matter
What the child did

Split second decisions
We had to make
At times it meant
A life we'd take

The people supported us
When we fought in Iraq
But when we came home
Some turned their back

And our employer the military
Made so many men sign
With promises of benefits
And "you'll have a good life"

Little did we know
The benefits would stop
When we needed them most
We felt so robbed

We made many sacrifices
And countless men fell
Some gave up their life
Others physical and mental
health

A kind word goes far
When you're in so much pain
Were our efforts appreciated
Or did we go through it in vain

The atrocities I saw
I carry so many bags
But I'd do it again
To protect the flag

One Thirty Eight

I died today you might
wonder how
So much time and energy
on others woes
Not stopping at the
boundary line
Sit down cuz here's
how the story goes

Once having such
empathic strength
Which eventually
became a curse
Grab a book and pick a page
Psalm 138 became
a healing verse

Though I read and don't
quite understand
And usually keep God
and religion at bay
In a way it changed
my future days
Perhaps I can paraphrase
or expatiate

God use your hand toward
the rage of my enemy
And preserve my
empathic being
Avenge for me those
who cause pain
And save me as I walk in
the midst of suffering

Your love it reaches
forever then more
Don't reject the
art of thy hands
Vindicate my need for justice
Against the brutality and
my ire of evil man

Take from me the
feeling of impotence
And remove the residual guilt
Of not being able to
make them pay
Instead let my heart at
ease be your will

The hatred of others
and their evil ways
Revenge no longer part
of my thoughts
I threw a dart and
prayed for strength
And an answer from
above is what I got

Enlightenment as
part of me died
But problems are no
longer my cross to bear
I just have to get out
of my own way
It doesn't mean that I don't care

How did that cause
me to die you ask
My thoughts and worries
given back to Him
No longer mine and
the relief I felt
I stepped aside so His
work could begin

Opiate Addiction

It started out innocent enough
It read take one or two for pain
Then one day things
suddenly changed
Like a switch got
flipped in my brain

It had me in it's satanic grasp
Though I knew I could
stop at any time
But somehow it had
all the control
And left me crawling
and chained behind

Soon the need became so great
it's appetite never satisfied
To feel that good
just once again
Actions driven by the mind

Requiring more and
different kinds
Never believing that I'd die
I had once thought it
safe from harm
After all it had been prescribed

Looking back and from above
I don't recognize who I became
A disaster of an
epidemic breadth
With waves of death,
destruction and shame

Despite the tears of
those who cared
It took over my good sense
T'where I had none at all
It built an apathetic fence

Each time life left in the
wretched hands
Of an iniquitous tribunal
A sentence of death
before my time
Captured by another funeral

It matters not rich or poor
Indiscriminate as to
its victims be
Mother Theresa or the Pope
Cannot outrun its callous reach

Penance

I've seen the sun set
for the final time
It's always His way
And never mine

He doesn't seem to care
When the devil enters in
It's like it's payback time
For a previous sin

And when bad things happen
To people who are good
It seems like He allows it
Simply because He could

And I rather doubt
That He cares there's suffering
It seems He rather enjoys it
And the tears that it brings

He is not a father
That cries with the kids skinned knee
He is just cruel
And lacks empathy

I could be wrong
But there's so much evidence
Perhaps I'm just angry
Better go do penance

Reaching Out

I don't understand
I don't see any sores
But I'm in horrible pain
What's going on Lord

You said there's two sets
Of footprints in the sand
You said you wouldn't leave
And you'd hold my hand

But it seems so much
Is falling on me
Perhaps you think
I've outgrown your reach

I may have been quiet
And you took that to mean
That I don't need your help
With anything

But the truth is
I've been so busy with stuff
So I understand
If you've had enough

But I'm still here
And I'm needing you more
Please hear me now
As I fight this war

Alone I can't win
I see now that's true
Don't give up on me
I won't give up on you

Silent Cries

You were young
And seemed happy enough
But now I know
It was all a bluff

Deep inside
You hurt alright
It became too much
So you took your life

We'll never know why
You took that act
But with yourself
You made a pact

Indeed the pain
From what you knew
Would last forever
The demons haunted you

No longer overwhelmed
Have you found the peace
That you needed in life
But couldn't see

You were strong
And you tried at life
But inside the battle raged
A futile fight

Unending wars
Fought over again
Just when one ended
A new war'd begin

The struggles in your head
And the silent cries
Carried on relentlessly
No relief in sight

You were courageous
And now I see
You were strong
When I thought you weak

You fought the battles
All by yourself
And all alone
You went through hell

You chose silence
And a solitary fear
But peace at last
When death was near

Your pain ended
And you stopped the fight
But mine began
When you took your life

Suits and Briefcases

On the fast track to nowhere
Getting high with laughter
Cuz it's all a joke gone wrong
Not realized until after

You see me standing there
I'm but a ghost
Not feeling alive in any way
More of a guest than a host

Hearing the clock tick
Feeling the anxiety
Never knowing why
Or just how to be free

The obsessions of the mind
Lead to the bodily acts
To numb the itch
Of the cold hard facts

Of which we are compulsed
To stop the senseless noise
That our heads can bring
When not playing with our toys

What once was all fun
Now but a memory
Holding your own
And hiding all the crazy

Taking a deep breath
And slowing it all down
A moment of sanity
Before the rebound

Who would ever think
That we could all be broken
When we face the world daily
With our many masks on

We all know and experience it
But don't show it on our faces
And we hide it well, though
With our suits and briefcases

Take a Walk

Walk in my shoes
Or look through my lens
When you think you get it
Do it all over again

Keep on and on
Until there's no doubt
You know who I am
And what I'm about

Wear my skin
And feel what I'm feeling
You may want to run away
Because it's not appealing

If you think what I think
And see what I see
In my shoes
You won't want to be

The grass is always greener
On the other side
Except when you experience
What's going on inside

The challenges are many
The joys are few
So look with your lens
And wear your own shoes

The Color of Darkness

The color of darkness
Is when you get to see
A glimmer of hope
A moment of clarity

But when you're at
That point in life
It's darker than dark
And there is no light

When you're at the point
Things are turning gray
And the color's fading
As you lose your way

The rods and the cones
In the eyes are no good
Cuz the color of darkness
Determines the mood

If you should wake
And not see black
It may mean
You're coming back

It may still be dark
But if you can see
You may be entering
Reality

You're coming along
When the gray is less
And you're feeling more
The color of darkness

The Dark Alley

In a dark alley
I fall to my knees
God oh God
Why have you left me

In my chest is an ache
And I'm in this place in my mind
I feel so alone
And I'm empty inside

My hands have felt the softness
That life can bring
But now my heart
Can't feel anything

You see I cared too much
For the many suffering
All the incessant worry
And the pain that it brings

Now I'm numb all over
And I want it to end
But I lack the courage
To transcend

So I cry to myself
At times there's no tears
And I'm always left wondering
Why He left me here

The Distracted Mind

Some say I have a distracted mind
At first I thought they were less than kind
But as time went on then I knew
What they said was oh so true

I'll have a goal and start the walk
But half-way there I start to talk
Then another turn and another thought
No matter how I fight the distracted thought

It comes to be that I no longer know
Whether I am going to or fro
I'm lucky I still know my name
Cuz nothing else is ever the same

Things change daily no routine
That's how it's been forever it seems
I get confused and sometimes scared
I pray for others their life be spared

I don't recognize me when I take a look
The story's new but it's the same book
Every day is new the things I find
Courtesy of a distracted mind

The Dormant Seed

The dormant seed
Had been waiting for years
To come to life
Now its end is near

It needed something to grow
A thing that it lacked
Though it knew lots of love
It was rather abstract

It was missing the one item
To perfect the soufflé
And without it
It just wouldn't be the same

That thing is different
for each and every one
We sow our own seed
And then we're done

Some get lucky
They get to watch it grow
Others
Will never know

It knows freedom
And it multiplies
But the dead seed behind
Is life defied

The Forgery

Who am I
Will I ever know
I'm a forgery
A facade I show

Can I remove the mask
And reveal me
In the meantime
I'm a forgery

You get to see
Who I want you to
But you have no idea
What I'm going through

Inside I die
At this fake life I lead
Why don't I show you
My reality

Is it that I can't
Or just don't know
Who I am
What I'm supposed to show

My forgery
It is my own
With myself
It's a contentious bone

I don't know how to stop it
Or be someone else
I'm so lost inside
This bed of kelp

I swim for freedom
And I come up for air
It's all a ruse
I'm going nowhere

The Game

It was just a typical day
Sunlight shining on the leaves
And the smell of wet concrete
After a night of rain fed the trees

We played the hokey pokey
And turned ourselves around
We played hide-n-seek
Until we were found

The monkeys bars
And merry go round
That's how we'd spend time
At the playground

Then came growing up
And things weren't the same
Soon there was no more
Playing of games

The responsibilities
And stress of decisions
Become the game of life
The impossible missions

And in old age
When you can no longer run
You remember that kid
That was having all the fun

When it's no longer fun
And no games remain
You take a deep breath
That's the end of the games

The Last Tear

The kid at the harbor asked his
grandpa
What does that mean
Grandpa said sit down I'll
tell you
And then you'll see

The cap'n he was a rugged sort
The kind that in a bar one
might fear
But he sat on a stool in the back
of the joint
And night after night he cried
into his beer

His crew they took to a bottle
of gin
But the captain wouldn't go
near it
He had a past with the hard stuff
And now swore off that spirit

For he had spent many a day
And often many nights
Drinking away his troubles
And wiping the tears he cried

This day started out as any other
The sun with a golden hue
The seas were calm and glistened
A far off horizon in her view

His boat was known as the Hell
and Back
Which summed up his lifetime
As his troubles and drinking
peaked
He became known and was less
than kind

Now on a roughened sea
With the rain coming down
He had been here times before
And knew he was hell-bound

As the night had fallen
The sheer curtain turned to black
The storm it kept right on coming
Now there was no turning back

Through the thirty five foot seas
She was tossed about
Thrown side to side in the ditch
He began to have his doubts

Right then a rogue wave
grabbed her
And pulled her underneath
the sea
The captain said a short prayer
As he held fast to the wheel

God I'm not a believin' man
But this is one I hope you hear
For if you save her for me
I promise no more tears

Somehow she had righted
herself
The storm it passed on by
And the frightened crew and
captain
Let out a grateful cry

Later on while back in port
And she was tied up to the pier
The captain made good on his
promise
As he christened The Last Tear

The Man With the Sign

They stand on the corner
And usually have a sign
They ask for money
Then sometimes go buy wine

There was this one man
He was dirty with filthy clothes
No one stopped to ask
How his story goes

"Go get a job and work like us"
Some drivers shouted at him
Never knowing his story
They passed him by again

Words they really hurt him
And cut him to the core
But he would simply stand there
He couldn't possibly hurt more

If you took a close look
You'd see a tear in his eye
He just stood by stoic like
No more would he cry

For years ago he made a
promise
His word was always good
For if he let his tears go
There would be a flood

Some handed him their spare
change
And some just looked away
Still others taunted him
And missed the point he tried
to make

If you have more than you need
Just give what you can
Perhaps the person with the sign
Is God and not a man

He may not appear as a bright
light
And He works in many ways
Just share a little kindness
For He gave you today

If you're one who feels anger
And perhaps you're less than kind
There could be more to the story
And to the man behind the sign

The Mind's Room

There is a room
To go within your mind
To change the scenery
Or go and hide

You can make it
What you want
A pleasant place
Or a place to haunt

Where you go
You decide
And you can change your place
Anytime

A place to be happy
A place to be sad
A place for fantasy
Or to drive you mad

When you cry
The last tear
There's no longer
Any fear

But remember
When you leave
Turn off the light
The room's empty

The Shoes

She gave her the shoes to walk in
They were small and
somewhat snug
She graciously thanked her
for them
She said you're welcome and
gave her a hug

He stopped and gave her his
jacket
It was bitter cold and snowing
outside
Without his generosity
I think she surely would have died

The teen approached then
stopped and smiled
She thought about what she
could do
She took off a mitten and gave
it to her
So that now she had two

The child walked by then
turned back
He took off the beanie he wore
He handed her the beanie
and said
Wear this to keep your
head warm

The first time in forever she was
comfortable
And she was able to sleep that
night
She dreamed of a beautiful
meadow
Not the daily struggle of her life

She wanted to stay in that
dream forever
Cuz in the meadow she was
running free
She had not a care in the world
She stopped running and sat
under a tree

The shade it felt so nice
Being under the warm sun
that day
She took in all the beauty
around her
So beautiful that she wanted
to stay

She then awoke and reality called
But she remembered the
freedom of her mind
That place had been so
magnificent
She couldn't wait to go there
another time

She arose and continued on
her way
Content with the place she was
able to find
And as the narrator I looked back
She had left her shoes behind

You see she had walked about
a mile
In somebody else's shoes
Which took her to an amazing
place
She wanted to share that with
someone too

The Twelve by Five

On the ocean
And I've capsized
The boat I was in
The twelve by five

Just one wave
Is all it takes
She rolled starboard
A grave mistake

Clinging to the hull
Left cold and wet
Flashes of life
Who could forget

The constant ire
And nagging words
The unspoken vengeance
That was never heard

The simple love
Not returned
When in her youth
Forever burned

The thoughts of innocence
And tracks they made
A memory
For another day

Is it all for the moment
Or yesteryear
Or times like this
When death is near

Through the salt water
And beyond the fog
Behind the eyes
The captain's log

Reel tape squealing
Memories don't lie
In your mind
'Twas the twelve by five

The "Wills" of Life

Will an anchor hold in a storm
Will the stars all fall
from the sky
Will I weather the storms of life
And come out the other side

Will the sky remain as blue
Will majestic mountains reign
Will a new day dawn with light
Or will everything
start to change

Will the suffering ever end
Will peace win the war
Will I see the goodness
in mankind
Or are some people
bad to the core

Will the oceans tide continue
Will clouds completely
disappear
Why is life a rabbit hole
Why am I filled with
so much fear

And why are streams drying up
Why is the air not clear
Why are birds falling
from out of the sky
Will we ever escape
this nightmare

Will the demons ever leave
Will people ever stop the hate
Will the trees stop standing
Or is it all left up to fate

Will the light go dark for good
Will the hurting ever end
Will the rainbows
lose their color
Will my broken heart ever mend

Will man ever really be free
Will the killing and
maiming ever cease
Will children and
animals ever be safe
Will there be everlasting peace

Will time stop ticking
as we know it
Will there always be a doubt
Is the suffering all for naught
Or will we ever get to find out

Today's Tomorrow

My heart is broken
My dreams have died
My soul has no will
My spirit cries

In the dark of the night
When all is calm
I lay there wondering
Should I go on

Is it a choice
When it's all gone black
And is there any
Coming back

Moving slowly
There is no more fight
I touch but don't feel
I see without sight

With a lions loud roar
My being cries out
Why doesn't He listen
What's this pain about

Every breath that I take
I inhale fire
No more songs
From the choir

I reach into the air
But He doesn't take my hand
Doesn't he know
I'm at my end

And as my fist clenches
I want all to know
The torture each breath brings
And it keeps on growing

PLEASE let it stop
Please, let it stop
I give up
To my knees I'll drop

Because my heart is broken
And I've cried my last cry
I'm but a shell
My soul has now died

Tolerance

I don't fit in my body
I don't fit in my head
Many times I've felt as if
I'd just be better off dead

Maybe I have low self-esteem
Maybe I'm depressed
Maybe I am fat or thin
Just give me some respect

Maybe I'm transgender
Maybe I am gay
Maybe I have green hair
What difference does it make

The other kids are mean to me
Some ignore that I exist
Others call me names
One hit me with his fist

Even though I may
not look like you
Or have the same accent
I'm still a human being
And I'm not any different

We may be political opposites
Which doesn't make
us right or wrong
We may like different music
But we need to get along

We are all born a certain way
And each have our own stuff
Don't pay attention
to the bullies
Life is tough enough

You're a special person
Know that you are not alone
If you need help, reach out
Til you feel at home

When Life Sucks

There are days
When life sucks real bad
Days of frustration
When you're angry or sad

And it seems
That nothing goes right
Even with yourself
All you do is fight

You just wanna give in
And kick something
Then you're left
With limping

So take a deep breath
And scream real loud
Just make sure
You're not in a crowd

At any time
You can start the day over
Or go to bed
And pull up the covers

Just let today go
Let all the crap be
Tomorrow's a new day
Wake up and breathe

White Collar Man

A white collar
A man of the cloth
Who'd suspect
He had a sinister plot

Dedicated to God
Obviously not
Concealed evil desires
Which he never fought

He prayed for young victims
And preyed on them too
They trusted him faithfully
As so many do

Taking advantage
Of ones who believed
He befriended the children
To service his needs

Once young and innocent
Now full of shame
As adults they still suffer
But the priest is to blame

Though all the survivors
Have been very strong
Some still feel
They did something wrong

You did nothing wrong
At fault you are not
For his evil ways
In hell he will rot

Walking Away

This is me walking away
This is me walking away

I turned my back there was so much pain
Realizing all of this was in vain

The sadness and fear felt by others
Made me believe You could not be bothered

For so long You were held up high
You were the ultimate guiding light

But now I see that there is no love
Coming from the Heavens up above

This is me walking away
This is me walking away

Why did You not answer me
When I went forth pleading to thee

Left to my own the darkened spirit rose
Telling me His love it comes and goes

We're not even here for a minutes time
Why does it seem that it's all a fight

When in our souls we believed strongly
Leaving our hearts totally empty

This is me walking away
This is me walking away
This is my back turned away from You
The way You turned Yours on me

CHAPTER FOUR

JEFF

Jeff

The road it may be lonely
You had made it a little less so
A kind word or a gesture
Maybe it was a simple "hello"

With you I know my
life was better
I'll forever remember our chats
Sometimes deep conversations
Other times just about
this and that

I didn't see you daily
But you made such
an impact on me
You taught me one of
my life's lessons
Perseverance in the
face of adversity

You were kind and sensitive
A warrior until the end
Unselfish and full of heart
I pray that you've found
peace my friend

A heavy heart is mine today
And as I light a candle for you
I'm grateful for your memory
Though your time
came way too soon

A sense of calm now
permeates the air
No rush of chaos to
get things done
A gentle giant can
now rest his head
Now that you are safe at home

With the wings of an angel
And the gentleness of a dove
You're at the right
hand of the Father
In the Heavens up above

And so I thank the universe
For the time you were my friend
Just save a spot on
a cloud for me
Until we meet again

Numb and Alone

I feel numb and alone
Since you took your life
Maybe that's because
I'll never understand why

I get the demons
That can haunt one's every night
And I know you fought the battle
Til you went into the light

As a candle shines
So does your memory
Though it fades with time
It's more important you're at peace

I have such unbearable pain
And my heart is broken
Turn back the hands of time
I long to see or hear you again

His Peace

In desperation you took your life
Now some say you'll go to hell
Others say you were weak
But I know the courage it took

The courageous act to leave the known
And go to the far side of nowhere
Where nothing's known and it's not in the Book
I pray you have no more fears

It was the same for many years
Nothing changing no more tears at least
You left so you could take a look
And see if you could find much needed peace

A look at what others cannot see
Where selfishness has no place
Upon the top you're granted peace
You're at the right hand you see His face

My Friend

My friend
I walk the lonely road
You knew it too
Then you had to go

In our hearts
We longed for peace
A little quiet
Let the canons cease

A jewelers jewel
An artifact
All the love in the world
Won't bring you back

Sounds have now dulled
Colors are not quite as bright
There's a longing in my being
And the emptiness doesn't feel right

But you're in my heart
Strong as you'd stand
You did the best
That anyone can

You charged through battle
Your role was clear
A gentle warrior
I'll take it from here

Though the heartache remains
And the pain continues
You were my buddy my pal my friend
And I'll never forget you

The Quiet Warrior

The quiet warrior
Who fought the galant fight
Honorable friend during the daytime
Tortured mind at night

The quiet warrior
Kept tears close to his chest
But an upstanding soldier
He was the very best

The quiet warrior
Just couldn't save himself
The battle was just too much
The warrior's inner hell

The quiet warrior
Fought silently for years
But now It's time to lay down the sword
I'll take it all from here

The quiet warrior
The battle has now ceased
The quiet warrior
Has finally found peace

The quiet warrior
Code of honor through and through
A courageous gentle giant
Anyone ever knew

The quiet warrior
Who's now part of the wind
A brave and gentle soul
Who was a loyal friend

Loss

There's this gut wrenching emptiness
From missing you
I don't know how to fill it
I don't know what to do

I go this way then that way
Nothing is right
I'm lost and confused
And have no insight

The pain is intense
As is the reality
You're gone from this earth
And not returning

Aw but I find solace
Holding you in my heart
And the memories in my head
So you're not very far

And when I feel down
And feel the huge loss
I remember you momentarily
And gone you're not

I Walk the Painful Path

I walk the painful path
In the wake of your death
It's hard for me fathom
It's hard to take a breath

I am numb yet I feel so much
Confusion at the helm
Stuck to the ground going nowhere
And totally overwhelmed

You were very troubled
And sought to find relief
While I go through hell
You have finally found peace

I am not angry or bitter
You had to slay your demons
I'm left alone and lonely
As I try to find a meaning

Meaning to why we suffer
Meaning to why some of us must leave
Please never leave my heart
And never leave me

My Friend Jeff

From the beginning
You were kind and sensitive
In a way you even taught me
How I should live

Staying in your own lane
Living in the 'now'
Always something to hope for
Even when you're down

There's unending possibilities
And you can always have hope
When faced with adversity
With others you can cope

You continued to teach me
Over and over again
Love and friendship conquer all
Even in the very end

Though weaker and
more fragile
Your resilience and
your strength
Taught me a great lesson
Of what life really meant

Always kind to others
And your unselfish way
You gave to me a gift
To live life each day

Now with the wings of an angel
The gentleness of a dove
You're at the right
hand of the Father
In the Heavens up above

I sense this total emptiness
That I feel over and over again
And although my
heart still aches
I'm blessed you were my friend

Chumash Mountain

I go to Chumash Mountain
And I sit atop a rock
That's when you came to mind again
You're always in my thoughts

A cool wind was at my back
And I felt I had no cares
As I looked down at the valley below
I knew that you were there

I thought that I could hear your voice
But it was just the breeze
In the Mountain resides your spirit
It too holds memories

A foot once stepped upon this land
Modern man and Indian too
But up on Chumash Mountain
I only think of you

I try to catch my breath
And from my face I wipe the tears
A sudden sense of calmness
And not a sense of fear

As the sun begins to set
And I begin my downward climb
I remember what I'm thankful for
That you were in my life

My Last Ride

I'm riding on my Indian
Leathers hittin the wind
God it's good to be back
On the road again

It's just me and my Indian
Back for one last ride
Me and my Indian motorcycle
Together one last night

No more wrenches or
screwdrivers
She's put back and feeling good
I begin my first ride by
gettin out
And turn left, free of the hood

There's no more rushing or
insanity
That chaos and confusion
where I lost myself
No more crazy ass neighbors
I wish would leave and go to hell

Yep I've got it all together
Facing life like it's a new day
Stand tall and take a deep
breath
Throw my leg over I'm on my way

On my way to nowhere
It's me and the open road
No plans or agendas
Just leavin that old zip code

That place where I became him
Him who wasn't me
That stressful dirt path to home
Never again, I'm on the road to
peace

I just keep on ridin til the third
sunset
Peace it is all mine
Eventually I arrive at freedom
Goggles dirty I get off the grind

I get to the gates at Woolsey
Canyon
But the sign doesn't say you're
being watched
It says peace to all who
enter here
I see a man dressed in all white
cloth

I musta taken a wrong turn
I should be able to see home
from here
He said my son you've reached
your home
Now let go of all your fears

I felt for a moment my helmet
was too tight
But then I saw my dad next
to me
Ugo and BOLO were there too
I had come home, indeed

215

Suicide is not glamorous. It hurts. It hurts and affects everyone you know and even those you don't know. The thought of suicide or dying or taking your own life may seem like the answer, may seem like relief, may even seem like a welcome alternative to whatever is going on or what you are feeling or going through. The thing is, most of the time choosing life instead will eventually bring about a change or shift or another answer that you will be comfortable with. And, perhaps, your sticking around is to benefit or help someone else, albeit difficult to see this at the time. Life is not always about you but what you bring to someone else, maybe someone you don't even know right now. Trust in this thing called life. It's been around for a very long time and our very nature wants us to live. Sure it may seem "easier" to submit to suicide then to continue with what the issue, problem, or feeling is. But if you fight and continue to fight and even fight again and again, and then fight some more, although you may be absolutely and completely exhausted there will be a shift. Perhaps this shift will not be immediately known to you and will be instead for someone else. But stay open to the workings of the universe and eventually you may see the beauty and goodness that you bring by choosing life.

Suicide wants you. Suicide uses you. Suicide controls you. Suicide tricks you. Suicide convinces you of things that are not so. Suicide wants to win. Period. Don't let it win! DO NOT LET IT WIN!

If you are feeling suicidal or sad or depressed or fearful or destined or defeated or desperate or like you are being called by it or feel like it's an answer or you just want to end it, tell someone, call a hotline, call the suicide hotline at **1-800-273-8255**, call a hospital, call 911 or text CONNECT to 741741 from anywhere in the USA, anytime, about any type of crisis.

Speak up. Do not suffer in silence. You are not alone. YOU ARE NOT ALONE. JUST DON'T DO IT. SURVIVE WHATEVER THE ADVERSITY IS. NO MATTER WHAT DO NOT GIVE UP. DO NOT GIVE IN. FIGHT!

CHAPTER FIVE

My Valley

I walk in the valley of death
Nearly every day
But I walk alone
I don't know any other way

Thy rod and staff do not comfort me
There's not anything that will
Why hast Thou abandoned me
Is it not Your blood to be spilled

We're to live by the golden rule
So what does it mean an eye for an eye
Are You our Savior
Or is it all a bunch of lies

The cup it doesn't pass me by
My head held high and never to fear
Weighted down with tears of blood
I've carried the cross for many years

A Group Now Gathers

I'm a prisoner of my thoughts
And I hold steadfast to their destruction
Not allowing a rational balance
Denial is not up for discussion

I walk for miles in my mind
Wearing out countless shoes
While trying to find some explanation
For the hatred and why man's so cruel

But there's no reason and I'm left empty
Left with nothing and quite numb
If you can go on after knowing truths
I guess then I'm the one who's dumb

I don't even know the beings I cry over
Honestly it hurts me to the core
But God I hope there's peace after this
Otherwise what was all this suffering for

The tears trickle for hours upon hours
Why so much suffering and so little good
I cannot avenge their evils ways
A group now gathers where I once stood

Sorry Seems To Be
The Hardest Word

A favorite show
A favorite song
All left to wonder
What went wrong

You feel the guilt
And the loss
And want to change the
outcome
At any cost

But it was all mine to feel
As I had the need
A want to fill the space
And to finally be free

And you're sad
Cuz it's not fair
The time we have or don't
On this earth

It's all temporary
Except the sorrow
Which seems to keep going
Right through tomorrow

Until the heart stops
and even longer still
The anguish continues
Our eyes with tears fill

A million little things
All add up to one
But there's no going back
To where we're from

There's no relief for some pain
Despite willing ears
That meet you with every step
And all your words they hear

The emptiness felt
Never gets filled in that spot
A vast abyss
That never ever forgot

You're either ok
Or perhaps not
Perhaps satisfied
With what you've got

Cuz it's a million little ones
That won't see the light of day
Because of other plans
Now the tears have their way

They pave the road
With should haves and
wanted to's
But fear got in the way
Now hope's too few

The cross to bear
Was torn apart
It was set ablaze
Doomed from the start

Where do you go
To escape the flames
You say sorry
And perhaps begin again

Sorry seems to be
The hardest word
That I've had to say
And that you've heard

A Walk Along the Trail

A walk along the trail
Up ahead a divide
Ponder it for a long time
Do I go left or do I go right

Left it seems easier
Paved and not so rough
But will it build character
Is the easy out enough

Right is incredibly rocky
A pothole ridden dirt road
This trail will surely build endurance
But is it the way I want to go

Both trails have been forged
By others before me
Perhaps I'll forge my own path
And go right in between

The Soul's Moirai

Grief of mind, body, spirit, soul
Feeling only anguish and despair
I reach up for the hand of God
I reach higher but don't even
feel air

Both hands reaching for Him
And up on my tip toes
Desperate to feel the Creator's
touch
I turn away because I know

He's not going to save me
Perhaps He doesn't care
Leaving me weeping in solitude
Not even a hint that He's there

Throughout this beings
existence
And all its' turmoil and pain
He's never seemed to be there
Empty prayers and dreams again

How much can one take
The flood's over my head
A life without His light and
grace
Leaves me lonely, empty,
and dead

If He cared there'd be an answer
But only crickets speak
The silence of His apathy
Speaks volumes and sets
me free

Knowing He's no longer
connected
I am the master of my own
Moirai
The future of my reality
Belongs to fate and not to faith

He gave up on me so I free Him
Not a word or prayer to be
exchanged
No miracle to be experienced
Life's Book forever changed

The Psalm of life an illusionists
guide
We're on our own on this earth
For when you reach out you
will find
The hand of God is just not there

My Scars

You can't see my scars
I carry them inside
And I hold them close
Proof of battles I had to fight

The pain it continues
But are they less of scars
When they're not seen
Is there a different bar

They may be invisible
And it doesn't matter which kind
Both physical and mental pain
Will affect the mind

The little things add up
And some I cannot avenge
It stays inside festering
Then something bad happens again

It all keeps multiplying
So much so I can't stand the pain
And I can't reach the evil doers
How can I, on earth, remain

I don't want to see or hear another story
Or know another ounce of suffering
I just have to know the peace
Of what the end of life will bring

The Bond

The bond cannot be broken
'Tis' like the circle that is the sun
The bond between us
Cannot be undone

Not even in death
Will our hearts part
I'll always carry you close
You are not far

The bond took years
To build and make strong
And it will remain
When we are both gone

Silent Agony

If you listen real hard
Perhaps you'll hear me
I don't always speak in words
My silent agony

I cry as I whisper
Tears of anguish I hide
While words of loathing and self hate
Speak quietly inside

I draw you into my wonderful world
And you think the marvel is real
But the only thing real about it
Is how I want you to think I feel

You may see the stifled wail
Or hear the mighty tears instead
Perhaps you'd feel the shuttering fear
Whatever, it is only in your head

Cuz you are only willing to experience
What's acceptable in your mind
Whether or not it's the truth
Comfort you search to find

It can be dark wearing someone else's shoes
Especially without a map or guide
Your senses telling you what you want to believe
Grab an Uber and enjoy the ride

Sleepwalking

It was sometime in the past
That I ceased to exist
Since then I've been
sleepwalking
Like a boat gone adrift

Going through the motions
Day after day
Feeling nothing but numbness
Though I could still feel the pain

A boat on the ocean
No motor to guide it's way
High seas and sharks around
Too difficult to want to stay

Close my eyes and walk around
Or open them but not see
A blindness without an injury
I walk in my sleep

Awake during the daytime
Not seeing what is there
Nothing looks back
from the mirror
Can i exist without a care

I wonder about a purpose
Is there such a thing
Is it always just the journey
Or is it a song that we sing

Is it what we're taught
Or what we seek to learn
Are there second chances
Or do we get what we earn

Anyway I'm sleepwalking
Through this thing called life
And I'm afraid of waking
So my teddy bear I hold tight

Secret Room

I found a secret room
In the corner of my mind
I can go there and hide
And leave the chaos all behind

In this secret room
Silence abounds
A calm and comfortable place
Where I can't be found

Some say I lost my mind
Maybe I just took a break
Maybe I'm just asleep
But I don't want to wake

Cuz in this secret room
I feel safe once more
And I can't be bothered
Because I've locked the door

From my secret room
One day I just might leave
But until that time
I'm where I need to be

My Twilight Zone

My demons can't be seen
My demons can't be heard
My demons cause distress
For which there are no words

It's like a recurring nightmare
Nothing left but grief
How did this happen
Joy stolen by a thief

Did I look away
Or simply close my eyes
When I should have
paid attention
Now I choose to hide

There was another route
I know it once was here
A broken pair of glasses
But now it's all too clear

The path is totally empty
Everyone's gone away
Was it all my doing
There's no one left to play

Is life a perpetual circle
And we have to go more rounds
To complete unfinished
business
Or so we can be found

But I am not lost
No more paths for me
My mind is very troubled
I just need relief

This is my twilight zone
Everything's black and white
What's real is a broken mind
And there's nothing left to fight

My demons can't be seen
My demons can't be heard
My demons cause distress
For which there are no words

Knock Knock

Can't you hear me knocking
I've been out here since quarter
of five
Like the man said in his 70's tune
I've got freedom but not
much time

Can't you hear me knocking
I'm still waiting out here
Why aren't you answering
the door
You know as I do my time is near

Can't you hear me knocking
Perhaps I'll walk right in
But will you hold that
against me
As you do my slightest sins

Can't you hear me knocking
Maybe I'll just break down
the door
Let me in and let's be done
Why are you making this so
much more

Can't you hear me knocking
Maybe I'll just pick the lock
I'm coming in one way or
another
So you might as well answer
my knock

Can't you hear me knocking
If I could I'd ring your bell
Maybe I'd have better luck
Knocking on the doors of hell

Can't you hear me knocking
Apparently it's not my time
But If I could I'd waltz right in
Don't you hear me I want to die

I guess you heard me knocking
Because you finally came out
But you told me to go on home
Then you turned me around

Defeated, I quit knocking
And down the ladder I began
to crawl
You said " I still need your help
while living"
Come back when I call

And so the moral goes
You never need to knock
And if you feel you do
Then perhaps it's time to talk

Talk to one who can help
If you're wanting it to end
He'll call you home soon enough
Then you'll walk up those stairs
again

So if you hear someone knocking
Take their hand to show you care
Help them through their
challenges
And gently guide them from
the stairs

Life and death on a continuum
And together we will walk
Through the good and bad times
Our arms will be interlocked

And when we hear His call
We'll walk to the door as one
Never alone again
The knocking will be done

Heart of the Matter

I went inside my heart
To see what it was like
To feel it's emptiness
And why it fights the fight

I felt the weight of the world
And saw the goodness of few
I heard the cries of many
The color was blue

It was not red like you'd think
And it was not full of life
It was full of heartache and pain
Agony, turmoil, and strife

My heart has been dissected
The chambers laid wide open
The inhumanity of man
Has left my heart broken

It sits there in pieces
Never to be repaired
Sensitive to nearly all
It's more than one can bear

Haven

So I retreat to where it's safe
By simply closing my eyes
All of a sudden the calm rains down
My armor builds as I hide

Hiding from life and all that's bad
My eyelids close and it goes away
And when it gets too much again
I find comfort in a gentle sway

A subtle rocking back and forth
And sometimes to the side
What you can't see won't hurt you
I tell myself with eyes closed tight

So nothing enters from underneath
A blanket tucked taut all around
A few la la la's to myself
Cannot hear another sound

What's not there in the dark goes away
Then behold you've aged with hair of gray
Bigger now and nerves of steel
But the feeling and fear it ever stays

Some things are not grown out of
Hiding isn't always closing your eyes
Knowing better and being stronger
Doesn't always end the fight

Running away may not be a solution
When fear goes deep and to the core
Clicking your heels won't bring you home
And for some things there's just no answer

Enjoyment

The good times may be many
Unnoticed, they simply pass by
But I find I wallow in the bad times
And with fun I'm so very blind

Blind to the joy that would be needed
When things get a little tough
And instead it becomes overwhelming
When do I say enough is enough

If I stock up on the good and positive
I'll be ready when things don't go right
And by storing up joyful experiences
When I have to I'll be able to fight

It may be hard to see the joy
But if I open my eyes
And follow my heart, mind, and senses
I might enjoy some of life's highs

Breathtaking

It's not an easy breath
Though it may be for you
It's a lifetime sentence
Not just a depressed mood

I may look like I'm a part of
This thing that you call life
And it may seem
that I am joyful
But I'm actually dying inside

The thoughts that go
through my mind
Are dark and not like yours
It's like I'm constantly armed
Getting ready for the
internal wars

Sometimes sad and
wanting death
Other times as high as can be
Maybe it's the voice in my head
Or the things that I
constantly see

Meds don't always work
And the side effects can be hell
Though at times I'm
in a good place
Other times I'm in a
deep dark well

You just don't know
what it's like
Living with a mental illness
Something that is not seen
But still remains among us

If it was a skinned knee
Or perhaps a black eye
You'd respect what I
go through daily
And maybe understand why

Why at times I may be quiet
Or preoccupied
Why each breath does
not come easy
And every day can be a fight

Curtain Call For a Lonely Soul

It's all just a stage
For some this is hell
A place we're stuck in
permanently
And forever have to dwell

Cuz this is the final act
The prolonged curtain call
Don't wait for another scene
It's over for us all

Those of you who aren't
finished
I'll see you on the other side
Take your time but let me go
You have your own train to ride

And some of you didn't know
You were going to the play
If you knew it was a one way
ticket
Would you have gone anyway

You who aren't ready
Try to escape
You can leave through the
back door
But it only leads to a repetition
of pain

A cycle of turns
Over and over again
Where you're going to
And where you've already been

Stop!
The insanity of it all
Now turn and bow
Before the curtain falls

"Twas the last act
And the last train is here
It'll take you from this station
To a place still so obscure

Climb aboard and take a seat
You are in for quite a ride
Round and round the railroad
track
It stops at the next act of
your life

Earth, it's the stage for your life
Where hope and dreams
collude
Enlightenment from the spirit
world
Your soul is forever renewed

One curtain opens and another
falls
You're the supporting actor in
your show
Just change the costumes and
the lines
It's all about letting your soul grow

Then one day it reaches its end
It's story no longer told
The actor faded away off screen
And all that's left is a lonely soul

Comfortably Numb

When I feel good
I notice all the chaos
But when I'm in the darkness
I don't feel lost

When in the dark
I feel at home
And I don't mind
When I'm alone

But with the light
There's too much to take in
It's mostly all bad anyway
And makes me crazy once again

You see the dark side
Makes me comfortably numb
And the light
Just isn't fun

When feeling fine
I'm aware of the suffering
It's in the lives of others
But to me, tears it brings

It's the sensitivity level
And I'm too sensitive
If something's bothering me
It's no way to live

So I choose my out
That is not the light
For me this choice
Is the one that's right

Forget any more good times
Tarnished with hurt and fear
To the dark I return
My friend is near

And should I choose further
To stop my breath
Don't cry I'm at peace
I find comfort in death

Always a Step Ahead

I move my pawn
You take my knight
Wherever I go
You steal my light

You keep things dark
Even during the day
I try to enjoy the sun
You block my way

I go for a swim
In the oceans waves
You put up a sign
Riptides, stay away

You invade and ruin
My every try
And weaken me so much
I don't ask why

You are always
A step ahead of me
You're more than a mood
Depression imprisons me

When will it stop
I don't know when
I think it's gone
Then it comes again

Always hovering
Waiting for the right time
To take its stand
And change my life

It's always there
Watching my every move
To ruin it all
When I'm in a good mood

It's takes over my life
When I lose the strength
And makes me believe
I can't go the length

It's all a cruel game
And like chess
It's checkmate my friend
When you're depressed

Indiscriminant

It doesn't have a voice of its own
But that doesn't make it less perilous
It can rear it's ugly head
And claim the very best of us

Sometimes we get a break
A summer vacation from our friend
Perhaps a fall to write home about
But then winter comes again

The darkness of depression
Non-discriminate in its attack
The thing that goes bump in the night
An invisible entity turning light to black

For something so clandestine
It can leave destruction in its wake
And in its height of puissance
One of sound mind it can take

If we give a voice to mental illness
And a vision to the invisible entity
Perhaps the strength of its madness
Will be lessened by our unity

A Day With the Devil

I was mad at God
So I wanted to see
What a day with the devil
Would be like for me

I got what I wanted
From my first request
I felt understood
And much less stressed

I was relaxed
And felt more in control
I got everything I wanted
Truth be told

My life was easier
With my new found friend
And I thought that I'd never
Want it to end

Ah but then it came time
To pay him back
And what I owed
Will leave you aghast

I was left with evil
Running my life
And it only got worse
The more i'd fight

My life is now his
An evil merry-go-round
Never escaping
And eventually hell-bound

I came out of it knowing
I'm better with the Lord
At least I know
He'll keep his word

Even though I go without
And my life is somewhat flawed
Keep the devil away from me
My life's in the hands of God

241

Letter to God

When I was young
I was taught to pray
When I went to church
And at the end of each day

I prayed not just for me
But the ones I loved
And even for the people
I didn't know of

But as I grew up
I prayed for toys or games
And later on
I prayed for no pain

When I got older
I'd try to bargain with You
What it was really about
I didn't have a clue

And when someone got sick
I prayed for their health
I learned it wasn't
Just about myself

Sometimes I'd pray
When I was mad
But rarely thanked You
When I was happy or glad

When a person would die
I would take knee and pray
For you to help them
Find their way

I felt a sense of relief
Knowing they were secure
And safe at Your right hand
For me it was all so obscure

Where Do They Go

How can it just end
When we take our last breath
Is it the end of life
And the beginning of death

How can they just be gone
Where do they go
What is the point
Of not letting us know

It happens so quickly
At times without warning
The end of one thing
Another's beginning

Does life go on
When the body dies
Is this the start
Of some other life

What do we know
About this earthly role
Are we a vessel
For a traveling soul

Is someone in charge
Of being so cruel
As to take our loved ones
Is it some kind of rule

Are we supposed to accept this
As a sacrifice
Of ourselves the survivors
Or the one who has died

When somebody passes
There's so much pain
It's too much to bear
Over and over again

There must be something more
There has to be belief
That's there's something better
When we're called to leave

Tyler Strong

I first met him
On a Saturday
I was watching tv
A football game

His name was Tyler
And he had a message for all
He may have been in a wheelchair
But he stood very tall

His team was the boilers
And they fought for Purdue
Fight til you can't
He inspired me too

Cancer may end up
Taking your life
But you beat cancer
By how you live that life

Live by his message
And his strength all along
Remember his courage
And live Tyler Strong

Turn Back the Clock

Turn back the clock
T'when but a kid
Hiding one's eyes
World ceases to exist

Back to being
That innocent child
And enjoy the journey
At least for a while

During that chapter
Not just a page
Whatever happened
Between kid and old age

An age I can't wait for
Since I was ten
A time when adulthood
Would finally begin

Invincible years
One has as a teen
A time of living
As one dares to dream

Then as an adult
Blink and it's gone
It's about old age
From now on

Friends and loved ones
Begin to die
Leaving you saying
I don't understand why

Then it hits
Soon will be my time
What ever happened
Cuz my life it went by

Thief

For the first time in my life
I couldn't catch my breath
You took the wind out of my sails
When you threatened me with
death

I was always able bodied
Healthy and strong
That was until
You came along

You were subtle and insidious
And snuck in like a thief
Once you were discovered
I could get no relief

You ate holes into my bones
And you were a pain by day
At night there was no relief
You wouldn't go away

No matter what I did
You kept taking more
And you kept taking until
I couldn't stand it anymore

You beat me down
My spirit broke apart
I tried to fight you
And I fought hard

But in the end I saw a light
Where you were not to be
A light from my Father
That's when I could see

It's not always about winning
Or having a stubborn streak
Or fighting a fight
It's about belief

It's staying in faith
And not having fear
It's knowing God the Father
Is very near

And when it comes time
To close my eyes
I'll know I won
For I left here a little more wise

The Rabbit Hole Is Life Itself

The rabbit hole is more
Than a hole in the ground
It is so much more
Something so profound

We think of the rabbit hole
As something so unreal
A maniacal way of living
Perhaps so we can't feel

Down and down we go
It is so insane
Often times we come out
Then go down once again

We are at a destination
Where we never arrive
And does that keep us
From feeling alive

Falling down the rabbit hole
What does that even mean
Some would say that it's life itself
Or so it would seem

The Ladder

The ladder
With its many rungs
Represents life
And it answers to none

Up you climb
When things are good
One at a time
And more if you could

But there's another direction
When things aren't fine
You struggle to ascend
But down you climb

You don't even climb
Rather you fall
Sometimes at the bottom
You have to crawl

When the darkness is thick
And you want to give in
Go up one rung at a time
Then do it again

The Class Bully

I may have been smaller
Than some of my classmates
I guess that's what contributed
To my eventual fate

I was always made fun of
And after school I was beat
They poured milk over my head
Who could be so mean

Their behavior only worsened
As the years continued on
We would go to lunch together
Then I turned and they
were gone

And on a daily basis
I was ditched at school
I guess the ring leaders
Thought this made them cool

I was no different
Than anyone in my grade
Maybe I was picked on
Cuz my parents didn't have it
made

Why did they disrespect me
Perhaps it was what I wore
It wasn't the latest fashion
But it was what we could afford

Now I'm an adult
But I still feel the pain
Of the child locked out of the
classroom
That had to endure all the rain

The bullies they don't care
About the trauma they inflict
And the damage that they do
When you're the last one to be
picked

Do unto others
We're taught that golden rule
There's no place for bullies
Or for those who are just cruel

Surrounded by Ire

Surrounded by hatred
And more specifically ire
In the middle a happy land
Beautiful forests caught in the
crossfire

Take a walk
On a safe inner path
Feeling the ills of the outer crowd
And their evil wrath

One can go on forever
In a forest of choice
Never knowing the outsiders'
Angry voice

You can hum to yourself
Or put your head on ignore
They're still on the outskirts
Knocking on reality's door

Stop denying what's there
As you hide behind a tree
Leave the forest behind
And finally be free

Go to a different place
Where people aren't mean
There's no need for a barrier
And they're not trying to get in

Where you can keep them out
And soar up above
Shake the scum off your skin
Be as free as a dove

It comes at a cost
You have to leave it all behind
The crap that's killing you
No more ire to find

Now you'll no longer know love
Or be able to be a part
Of those things you enjoyed
You chose a different start

A start that could be dark
Or may not even exist
But your anger was toxic
And away you had to get

They pushed you to it
Because of their sorted ways
Now you've permanently
Gone away

Staying in the Now

Are we just a tin man
Lion or scarecrow
Are these really parts of us
Or just characters in a show

Are there flying monkeys
Or clues we need to find
Is the poppy field really magical
Or is it all just in our mind

And the ruby slippers
Can they take us
somewhere else
Does the man behind
the curtain
Remind us of ourself

The beautiful good witch
And the bad witch that did melt
Maybe it is all about
The feelings that we felt

Is it all a dream
Maybe we're pawns
upon a board
Perhaps we're not even real
Is there a hidden door

A door to find the answer
Or at least to find a clue
To what we're doing here
The truth behind me and you

Is what we see
Just viewed in our mind
Maybe when we stop breathing
That is when we'll find

We get to begin our life
When we gasp for
that last breath
And only do we start to live
When the memories
end in death

Is this just a preview
To actuality
The mind's views, thoughts,
and memories
A prelude to eternity

The door to the universe opens
Only when our mind conceives
But what of those less fortunate
Do they know reality

How do we know for sure
I don't think we ever do
For now it's the reality
What's in our minds view

For this life we must be satisfied
Although a little bit perplexed
Stay in the now and live this life
Until we're called to what is next

Soul's Story

What is your soul's story
What does it want to say
Did you fulfill its wishes
Or did you throw it all away

We all make choices in life
But who are those choices for
Are they for us or are
they for others
Does that leave the soul
wanting for more

Will our soul be happy
When it goes its own way
Will there be unfinished
business
To make it come back some day

He thought he was
just a simple man
Uneducated and
mostly missing out
But one day he fell for a girl
And the rest took place
upon a cloud

Games of 'can you see me'
Games of 'your it' now
Finding what makes
each other happy
Kissing passionately
beneath the clouds

Previous thoughts
forgotten instantly
Their way of life changed
in an moment
It was now just the two of them
Would it be happiness
or must lament

Giving all your heart to one
And getting back the same
Does that tempt fate
to interrupt
Or is your soul to blame

If you're honest with yourself
And allow the soul's
story to be told
You'll be happier with yourself
And perhaps be satisfied
when growing old

Rita (A dedication)

Fight till the battle's over
That is what she did
Right until the end
And ever since she was a kid

Though there were times of trial
Still her faith always won out
For her service to
God and family
Was what life was about

A strong woman
through rough times
And she certainly had her fill
But she'd drop to her
knees in prayer
Because she knew it was His will

The epitome of perseverance
Glamorous inside and out
Her children first
along with Christ
Her love it left no doubt

Truly an inspiration
From the first time that we met
Stoic and brave instilling hope
Through prayer and
words she said

They called her a prayer warrior
With dedication to the Lord
A benevolent friend and mother
Guided by His word

And in those final hours
In the face of arduous agony
Her body weak yet
she stood strong
When He called and
she had to leave

No worry or pain she
has her wings
And her assignment has begun
For she is now in Heaven
With her Father and her son

Pause and Review

Take the load off your feet,
Sit down and relax
Close your eyes for awhile
And take a look back

You're always too busy
And moving so fast
You never take a minute
To review your past

What got you to here
To this place and time
All went so quickly
Now pause and rewind

Remembering how you felt
When with your true love
Knowing that's gotta
be the feeling
That Heaven's made of

And throughout your lifetime
There was some
heartache and pain
You wanted to share it
But no one ever came

That was getting you ready
For something bigger than you
When would it come
Nobody knew

When you open your eyes
You're not tired anymore
You feel centered and strong
Fearless, you open the door

To get where you need to be
And let it all in
Perhaps reviewing your journey
Is where you need to begin

But you have to slow down
Yielding at times for a rest
Before the sign posts
on the road
Become the stone for your head

Paradise

Are the stars
In the sky
Still up there
When it gets light

The stars will shine tomorrow
The sun will rise and set
The moon will show on most nights
There's no need to fret

Life will always have its challenges
With demons to conquer in the mind
Try to overcome and adapt
Cuz there's no chance to play rewind

You don't want to leave this earth early
And at times you'll need to fight
You have the strength within you
Like the darkness that contains light

Sometimes we ask why we're here
And question why we exist
Especially in times of turmoil
When pain and suffering persist

The answer lies beyond us
And beyond our ability to comprehend
Just believe there's a reason
And paradise if life ends

My Mom

I found comfort in your arms
From the very day I was born
I've always felt loved and safe
You were my umbrella in a storm

We had some difficult teenage years
But as we aged we were more like friends
We'd talk often but not enough
What I wouldn't give to converse again

You were always there no matter what
And you bandaged more than one skinned knee
And for those painful matters of the heart
You were always there for me

From now on my heart won't be the same
Neither will my birthdays be
That was always our special thing
But now you've got wings and you're at peace

You sit on a cloud still worrying
Always being the good mom
Go now be with your Father above
We'll be ok even though you're gone

He chose for you to come home
We were never promised a tomorrow
But I thank him for my mom
The lovely gift He let me borrow

You Just See
What I Portray

I'm withering away inside
Though I may be a light to you

Each day is a struggle
And so hard to get through

Life is not a challenge
For me it's a painful plight

I can't escape the torment
Though every day I try

Existence takes all my energy
And I feel so much despair

At times I can't get out of bed
And some days I just don't care

But I don't show you how I feel
You just see what I portray

Though there's no life in my eyes
And my soul is on its way

I let you see contentment
While I really feel confused

I still go through the motions
And laugh along with you

I may not isolate
And at times I may have fun

But inside I am dying
And I just want to be done

My thoughts have now
gone dark
And away from life I run

As I suffer alone in silence
And I don't tell anyone

What I used to see in color
Now I just see in black and white

I close my eyes and I'm
comforted
I see the end in sight

I can't explain the bliss I feel
As I no longer have to fight

No longer numb with apathy
I can finally see the light

Voice of Mental Illness

It doesn't have a voice of its own
But that doesn't make it less perilous
It can rear its ugly head
And claim the very best of us

Sometimes we get a break
A summer vacation from our friend
Perhaps a fall to write home about
But then winter comes again

The darkness of depression
Non-discriminate in its attack
The thing that goes bump in the night
An invisible entity turning light to black

For something so clandestine
It can leave destruction in its wake
And in its height of puissance
One of sound mind it can take

If we give a voice to mental illness
And a vision to the invisible entity
Perhaps the strength of its madness
Will be lessened by our unity

Life Isn't Always Happy

Life isn't always happy
Nor can we always cope
But things can only get better
When we have a little hope

Do the clouds ever disappear
Or do we just stop noticing
Does the music seem to stop
Or did we just stop singing

Are we really by ourselves
Perhaps wishing for a family
Do we get lost in a crowd
Or are we very lonely

Do we think others won't understand
Are we afraid that they'll taunt us
Do we just need to take care of ourselves
And not think about the stigma

Is all of life but a dream
A trick of the subconscious
Questioning was it real or not
Reality does haunt us

Free Yourself

Free yourself
Don't be owned by anyone
Free yourself
Take a stand and be as one

Free yourself
From the mental ball and chain
Free yourself
So you won't be hurt again

Free yourself
From that which keeps you from seeing
Free yourself
And become an empowered being

Free yourself
And do what you need
Free yourself
And forever be free

Free yourself
From that which holds you back
Free yourself
Face the fear and attack

Free yourself
Now and don't wait
Free yourself
Before it's way too late

Forgive Me

Can you forgive me
For what I put you through
You went through hell
I was addicted you knew

You wanted me to stop
And you even prayed
I told you I'd stop
The promise I made

But I couldn't stop
On my own I tried
I continued to use
Till the day I died

I regret from above
That it was you to find me
That isn't something
Anyone should see

Now you live with guilt
Cuz to God you prayed
If it be His will
Please end my pain

No need for guilt
You did what you could
But I had a disease
And by me you stood

If I could do it over
I certainly would
Of all in my life
You were so good

I'm up above watching
But from your life I am gone
Please work through my death
And then move on

No need for fear
Guilt or pain
I believe that one day
I'll see you again

Dissociation

I feel like I'm fighting
Something that I can't see
Maybe I'm really
Just fighting me

I'm fighting myself
From head to toe
But why I'm fighting
I don't really know

I fight the good parts of me
And I fight the bad
Trying to find the real me
Perhaps I never had

Has it always been this difficult
Finding my true self
Or has it been insidious
And even quite stealth

Sneaking up on me
When things are going good
Questioning a subtle change
In my current mood

Fight the need to sleep
It's just a waste of time
Until sudden exhaustion
For my body and my mind

It seems like nothing ever
changes
So sometimes I want to quit
It's as though in this body
and mind
I really just don't fit

Something is off
I'm just not comfortable
My mind says I'm sad
I feel in trouble

Why can't I be ok
And go along each day
Without giving any thought
To how to play the game

With a roll of the dice
I can move ahead
Or perhaps pick a card
That says rejected

Rejected from life
Or do I reject what I feel
Never really knowing
What part of me is real

Dissociation
Who decides what is real
and true
When does this game end
And who decides the rules

Different

She was a little different
We knew it right away
She had a target on her back
From the very first day

It was during the school year
And we were all quite young
And speaking for myself
I was pretty dumb

She wore Coke bottle glasses
Her brother too was slow
We preyed on them as they
walked home
The impact I didn't know

I had felt like a victor
And the bully in me felt strong
I wasn't brought up to fight
And I knew that it was wrong

I can't remember the time that
followed
I'm only haunted remembering
that day
Little did I realize
I'd contributed to her fate

Throughout the future years
She had met many more
like me
Some they just ignored her
Others she couldn't flee

It must have all weighed on her
greatly
Because before her time she died
I live with the guilt of that
fateful day
She died from suicide

I pray her trauma's ended
And to a beautiful place she went
Because I in part took from her
When I labeled her different

We all have to be accountable
For how we act and what we say
We may do damage for a
lifetime
And not just for a day

I just hope she rests in peace
And I pray for others everyday
Cuz no one should be a victim
Of another's hate and rage

Forever I'll live with the memory
And I'll never have any peace
That is my lifetime penance
For the day I chose to be
so mean

I don't know why we can't get
along
And with others just be kind
We're more alike than different
Why can't differences be blind

Dad

I see you lying there
And I can't remember when
The last time was
That I held your hand

I'm grateful for the chance
If I didn't get to before
To tell you how much you mean
And to hold your hand once more

I lean over your bed to whisper
As your strength begins to wane
There's a tear in your eye
You're tired and in pain

When you need to close your
eyes
It'll be okay
Go on up ahead with Him
Be strong and not afraid

Now you're spending time
On a cloud up above
With the wings of an angel
The gentleness of a dove

You'll always be here
In my heart and thoughts
And I'll never forget
The brave battle that you fought

I'm so thankful for our time
Even though you had to cross
My cherished memories
For when I'm feeling lost

The sun's not quite as bright
Even though my faith remains
I may have lost a gift
A gift that Heaven has now
gained

And if those days of darkness
Should ever come my way
I'll look up to the Heavens
and begin to pray

Help me through these days
When I become sad
And take away my tears
I just miss my dad

A Shadow, A Soul, A Stage Oh My!

Are we the creature or the shadow
Walking down the street
One is not without the other
Whatever happens when the two meet

Is it a shadow or is it a soul
That stands firmly on my back
Patiently waiting for me to ascend
While going round on the track

And when the doors are all closed
That which stops your stride
Take a step toward giving up
A soul is left where the body lies

It's the shadows of my soul
Like a lifelong bridge
Keeping me on the straight and narrow
Will father time ever forgive

For the shadow is my soul
It keeps me company and keeps me warm
Though I choose to go off script
Will it still take me to the next of doors

The doorway to tomorrow
Not like that of today
But something more everlasting
The soul on stage in a human play

A Reach Into Yesterday

As I climb through the mental
jungle gym
I am reminded of the
geometric dome
Making something out of
nothing
And spending time away
from home

Time away from myself, my
home
It's like mental metal bars
And making a new narrative
All to take you from where
you are

Climbing on that contraption
Making our life stories along
the way
Waiting to hear the keys of fear
Hoping to live another day

It takes me from what I'm doing
To a time and place of bliss
A time when I was a kid in a void
A time I greatly miss

A void of 'everything's possible'
Except when the lights go out
Then it's time for reality
As I'd become homeward
bound

Stomp and splash makes a
perfect day
With a Pooh Bear at your side
Somehow growing up as I did
Was worth the knock down
drag out fights

Now up in the age of adulthood
I tell my story as I can
Though now I try to harden my
heart
But I still try to hold your hand

You've left me here and
wondering
Will I e'er see you again
Just like the times of yesterday
Where my reality begins

You're the guide, the
enlightened voice
The experience of truth
That of which is lost to years
Except when in our youth

When did you leave me where
did you go
Wake up from your
slumber now
Because we have a story to tell
And alone I don't know how

Back to that play yard
jungle gym
Real or not it makes my
mind spin
I try to reach into yesterday
Oh to be that child again

A Corner of Light

Caught in a tiny dark corner of life
Knowing my mind isn't what it used to be
Seeing evil spirits at night
Though I plead they just won't leave

Feeling the evil all around
The thought of people being so cruel
I take up my dagger and arm myself
But I'm without energy to do the duel

Taking a breath is all I can do
A peaceful existence is beyond hope
Bad thoughts ricochet in the full mind
Curled up in the corner I cannot cope

I try to gel to find some peace
Maybe the universe can find compassion
Relax I can't there's so much clutter
I close my eyes searching for my ration

My ration of harmony is all I ask
Nothing more or less just to be in synch
There's something elusive in this life
That has to be the missing link

Searching through the dots and color
And beyond what closed eyes can see
The mountains reach above the clouds
And the rivers flow majestically

Trees of green and blue-gray skies
Deer are safe and running free
If I could just stay here with my mind
I believe I've found harmony and peace

Printed in the United States
By Bookmasters